On the †

To Marilyn,

With my prayers to
St. Thérèse for you and for
all your intentions.

In her love,

TO LIVE OF LOVE

Spiritual Spa

with Saint Thérèse of Lisieux

Angelina Muñiz-Liedo

© Copyright 2023

by Angelina Muñiz-Liedo

ISBN: 9798392169870

All rights reserved Mexico City, 202

ACKNOWLEDGMENTS

I dedicate this book to Our Lord, who is the love of my life, my companion, and the inspiration of all I do. I also want to dedicate it to Our Lady, who has been the cornerstone of *"Vida Humana and Lumen Vitae",* our ecclesial movement in favor a God´s life in our world.

This book is also a special token of appreciation to Saint Thérèse of Lisieux, in the 150th anniversary of her birth, the 100th anniversary of her beatification, and the 25th anniversary of her nomination as Doctor of the Church. I thank her deeply for being present in this book to touch the hearts of the readers through her spiritual teachings on God´s immense love.

My gratitude goes to the priests, friars, nuns, and lay people who have guided, accompanied, and followed me over time. Thanks to my friends and members of "Vida Humana and Lumen Vitae" for their faithfulness to our mission in favor of God's life in the world, and for their love and prayer.

 I also dedicate this book to my dear family, friends, and students, and to all those who in different ways have contributed with their knowledge, photographs, videos, and music, to the publishing of this book making of this project a beautiful reality, not only mine but ours.

This spiritual spa is dedicated in a special way to you, my reader whether I already know you, or you come as a new gift in my life. Everything I have written carries my prayer for you, thanking God for the miracle of your life and for opening your heart to let yourself be guided by Him, and by Saint Thérèse, on the path that will take you to the high peaks of the fullness of life.

Angelina Muñiz-Liedo

Table of Contents

PREAMBLE 9
   How to read this book 9
   What is a Spiritual Spa? 12
   In Search of Light 13
   The Art of Receptivity 14
   Some of the initial questions for you: 16
   Silence: The Language of Love 16
   Ten tips for preparing your spiritual spa 18

INTRODUCTION 23
   Interior Prayer: Place for the loving Encounter 23
   Beauty: a reflection of God´s glory 26
   The call and the answer 27

PART ONE 31
   "Spirit of God, fill my life" 31
   The Eclipse of God in Modern World 33
   Hope for the world 40
   St. Thérèse: Your great spiritual teacher 45
   Some Data of St. Thérèse 48
   Saint Thérèse´s Family 49
   The Virgin´s smile 51
   Story of a Soul 54
   Psychology of Caresses 55
   The Little Way of Spiritual Childhood 62

The Gospels: God's love letters 63
What is the Little Way of Spiritual Childhood about?............65
Our Desires..66
The story of Ryan Hreljac 67
Our limitations: opportunities for triumph 69
Time for prayer 73
The Rhythm of Prayer...73

SECOND PART 77

God does not ask of us something impossible 77
St. Thérèse, the saint of immense desires.............................79
My vocation is Love 81
I want an elevator to go to Heaven 83
Called to be saints 85
The great paradox 86
Self-acceptance 87
The process of conversion and sanctification 90
"Yes": the most important word in the Gospels...................95
The need to be humble..97
Questions for your reflection..99
The light of the Word of God 100
Jesus´s little bird...102
Remaining in Jesus ´s love forever 119
Time for prayer 120
New desires..124
Prayer in honour of St. Thérèse 126

PREAMBLE

How to read this book

"To live of Love" is a book written specially for you. It is not only a book to read, reflect, meditate, and pray. It is also an interactive and smart book to give you tools that will enrich and develop your human and spiritual life. It can also help you to start preparing yourself to become a spiritual guide for those, who could be interested in carrying out this Spiritual Spa with you.

Through these pages, you will find a series of links and QR codes with audiovisual material to enjoy videos, poems, beautiful music for your prayer times, and information about the life and work of Saint Thérèse of Lisieux.

This spiritual spa can be done according to your time and circumstances. If possible, I recommend that you take a week retreat, or one or two weekends. It will be very convenient for you to change your environment, get out of routine, and go to a place that offers you the possibility of being in silence and stillness. Choose a place where you will enjoy nature, and don´t have interruptions. Choose a space that you like and motivates you to discover the treasures you carry within you and let the light of the Spirit of God come to you.

If you can't do it this way, don't worry, you can also do it at home, at your own pace, according to the time you have. Read the book as if it were your daily companion waiting for you to enjoy and savor the message it contains, and letting it penetrate and nourish your spirit.

I specially recommend you prepare it very well. When you read the book, don't do it in a hurry or amid noise. To enter your inner self, it is essential that you leave everything else aside and give yourself the gift of being within you alone. If you prepare this spiritual spa carefully and dedicate quality time to it, I am sure that the Holy Spirit will come to you, give you many insights, and your life will be enriched in all aspects.

This is a spiritual spa that wants to enamor your heart through the most loving gaze of Jesus, who will change your darkness into light, your sadness into joy, your sorrows into new possibilities so that you will become fully alive and have a meaningful and joyful life.

This book could also be used as an evangelization project. All I share you can use it as a manual that could not only enrich you but others. So, I invite you to open your heart to the great adventure of God's love manifested in Jesus and let Him show you the special project He has for you.

You will go hand in hand with Saint Thérèse of Lisieux, whom we affectionately know as Saint Thérèse of the Child Jesus, or the Little Flower. She will guide you softly, sweetly, wisely, and lovingly on her "little way of spiritual childhood."

Silence and stillness will be your best allies and the first two conditions to enter your inner self. That is why I ask you to prepare a special place where you can enjoy being alone with the One who awaits you and who desires to meet you, love you and be with you in every encounter that you prepare to be with Him. He now, calls you, waits for you and says:

"Come to me to live of Love!"

****

What is a Spiritual Spa?

You may be wondering about the title of this book... The term "Spa" comes from Latin, which means "health through water." It is associated with treatments from mineral springs that have healing powers. Today, "spas" have become popular all over the world. They are beautiful places designed for rest and restoration, where visitors receive treatments for body care, massages, special diets for detoxification, relaxation and meditation exercises, thermal baths, and beauty products for the skin.

Our Spiritual Spa, as the name suggests, is something like this, but it goes straight to the source of living water, which is the Holy Spirit, doctor of our body, soul, and heart. His healing power will reach you and change whatever needs to be changed. It will restore your strength and give you all the treatments you need to detoxify your inner self, nourish you with the Word of God, relax you through meditation times, and unite you with Jesus in prayer.

Throughout the book, you will find many questions to learn more about yourself and help you grow both humanly and spiritually. It is essential that you take the time to go deep into them, so you receive the benefit of purifying and beautifying your life through the Holy Spirit´s dynamic action.

I invite you to immerse yourself in the living water of the Holy Spirit, and by doing so, find new ways to develop a more intimate relationship with Jesus, who is the *"fountain of life" (Ps 35)* and wants to fill your life with grace and blessing.

In Search of Light

Mystics of all beliefs have always sought the light and fullness of spiritual life. Illumination and fullness are not just for mystics or a few, but for also for you, me, and everyone.

It is the light of God that, like a luminous beacon, illuminates us on the path of life so that we do not run aground, but come out of darkness and see where we are and where we are headed.

The light I am talking about is not just any light, but nothing less than the light of God, which **gives us the energy to live each day and leads us to fullness.** Jesus confirms this by saying:

"I am the light of the world. Whoever follows me will not walk in darkness but will have the light of life." (Jn 8:12)

The Art of Receptivity

Now that you are starting this Spiritual Spa, I invite you to continue your journey toward the light, practicing the art of receptivity. **Slowdown** and follow the natural rhythm that I advise you **so that gently, without haste, you become receptive** and welcome everything that the Holy Spirit inspires you. Our Spiritual Spa is a wonderful opportunity to enter within yourself, where God dwells at the center of your heart, and where most secret things happen between Him and you.

Being receptive means trusting and letting God take the initiative. Like a beautiful flower opening every day to receive the morning dew and sunlight, allowing itself to be nourished, cleansed, and beautified, so it becomes what it has been created for.

This receptive attitude is that of **welcoming the mystery of God within you.** This will impel you so that the life and love of God become increasingly real in yourself, to receive the dew and the sun of his infinite love for you, **present in your life always, and forever.**

I also call this spiritual spa, a spiritual retreat, as it wants you to **withdraw from the everyday hustle and bustle and** invites you to give yourself this privileged time in which the **Holy Spirit will pour his gifts in you,** so that you realize the value of your person, and rejoice in knowing that **you are immensely and unconditionally loved by God.**

It is **Jesus who also wants to seduce you** with his steadfast love, **to make you fall in love with Him, awakening in you the desire and determination to follow Him** in the unique, unrepeatable, and formidable **project He has for you**, and which will lead you without a doubt, towards the light and fullness of your human and divine life, **which is nothing other than holiness.**

Some of the initial questions for you:

* What made you decide to do this Spiritual Spa?

* What does taking this time mean to you?

* What attracts you?

* What do you need to reflect on?

* What are your expectations?

* What would you like to say to Jesus?

* What do you want to ask of him?

* What do you want to offer him?

Silence: The Language of Love

The answers to these questions can be found in the silence of your heart. Silence is the language of love, as we read in the Scriptures:

"I will lead her into the desert and there I will speak to her heart." (Hos 2:14)

It is in silence that God inflames the heart by entering the soul into the *"silent music, the sounding solitude, the supper that refreshes, and deepens love."* All this will revive and enkindle love. As *St. John of the Cross* speaks of in his **Spiritual Canticle.**[1]

By entering silence, you will realize that your inner self will gradually awaken, and you will experience the loving presence of Our Lord in your heart, intimate center of your being.

---

[1] The Collected Works of St. John of the Cross. ICS Publications, Washington D.C. third Edition p. 470

Now that you are beginning this great adventure, prepare yourself to **enjoy it by abandoning yourself in the love of God**, knowing that the Lord and St. Thérèse, they know what you need, accompany you in your journey, and are with you to **surprise you with the wonders of their love.**

Ten tips for preparing your spiritual spa.

As I mentioned to you before, the key to greatly benefit from this retreat, is to prepare it well, as you would for meeting with a dearest friend. Jesus is someone who loves you like no one else can, so **make of your retreat an encounter with Jesus, one filled with intimate friendship, affection, and great love.**

1. Find a special place. It can be in **your home or another place** where you feel comfortable, inspired, and where you can be alone and in silence.

If you live with family, let them know of your desire to have this quiet time and ask them to respect your space and silence. If this is not possible, find another suitable place for meaningful solitude.

2. Be creative. Whether you decide to do this retreat at home or elsewhere, choose a place in your home, that you may turn it into your private little chapel. You can set up a small altar with a crucifix, an image of Jesus that you like, an image of Virgin Mary, and a picture of Saint Thérèse. You can also decorate your altar with candles, flowers, a Bible, a Rosary, some beautiful music, or something else that is special to you.

To have a special little place to pray at your home will be an excellent way for you to give honor and praise Jesus, Mary, and Saint Thérèse.

3. Change your pace. Live this spiritual spa without haste, relaxing, resting, breathing freely, **emptying your mind of negative thoughts** that unsettle you, **without worrying about other things,** so they don't distract you.

4. Prepare your mind and heart. If you have decided to take this retreat, it is because **something has caught your attention about it.** Maybe you have thought that you need it. So, **ask yourself what you would like to achieve**, what you need to say to Jesus, Saint Thérèse, Virgin Mary. What do you want to ask them to help you enrich your life, your relationships with others, with yourself, and with God.

5. Have a notebook and pen on hand to take notes that are important to you. This will be useful, not only during the retreat but also afterwards.

20

Writing your answers, reflections, and intuitions you may have received from the Holy Spirit will be a beautiful memory that you can keep in a special place so that **when the retreat is over, you can always return to them to remember and refresh** your experiences and the points that were most important to you.

6. Start your retreat with the suggested Holy Spirit video. Listen to it in a **prayerful mood** and ask Him to enlighten you throughout the retreat. **The Holy Spirit is your inner teacher in charge of inspiring you.** He is eager to give you His gifts and encourage you to develop them so you can put them into action. Open the ears of your heart and listen to Him carefully. Do this throughout the whole retreat when I give you videos, poems, or music to meditate and pray.

7. Ask Virgin Mary to accompany and bless you. As your Mother in heaven, **she will be interceding for you and guide you to follow her beloved son Jesus more closely**. She will help you to put into practice the graces and blessings you receive from both.

8. Approach Saint Thérèse of the Child Jesus. She wants to be **your guide, spiritual teacher, and friend**. She will teach you in a very simple and practical way **how to discern what God**

wants for you and will take you by the hand to confidently follow her spiritual path.

9. Open your heart to God. This is the **most important thing**. Listen to what there is in your heart, the desires that you have and want to become a reality. Make yourself available to receive the love of Jesus, of Our lady, and of Saint Thérèse. **Be certain that they want to fill your current life with grace and blessings.**

10. Pray for all your loved ones, for those who, like you, are participating in this Spiritual Spa, and please do not forget to pray for me as well. **Remember that union is strength.**

When we pray for each other, the power and love of God pour out abundantly on all of us. Let us pray together so that we may emerge renewed from this experience, becoming better people for our own good, for the good of our loved ones, for the glory of God, and for the salvation of many.

I wish you a great Spiritual Spa

You have my prayers!

INTRODUCTION

Interior Prayer: Place for the loving Encounter

Years ago, in a course I took on techniques of interior prayer at the Spirituality Center of the Missionaries of the Holy Spirit in Mexico City, I discovered important teachings about this kind of prayer through the book *"Cinq soirées sur la prière intérieure"* by Father Henri Caffarel,[2] a well-known French priest in Paris, who founded the Groups of Our Lady and dedicated himself to giving retreats on interior prayer.

Castle of Troussures

---

[2]Feu Nouveau Editions 1988. Paris, France

I loved the course, and after completing it, I became most interested in the subject, so, I started practicing, and researching more about interior, silent and contemplative prayer.

Providentially, some time later, I had the great opportunity to go to France and participate in one of the *"Weeks of Prayer"* that Father Caffarel led at the small Castle of Troussures, located in the beautiful French countryside north of the country, where Father Caffarel lived and offered these *"Weeks of Prayer."* That wonderful week sparked in me a greater interest in interior, meditative, and contemplative prayer, and **opened the door to the path of growth in my spiritual life.**

When I returned to Mexico, immersed in the topic of prayer, I learned from a friend about the existence of "*Carmel Maranatha House of Prayer*" in Valle de Bravo, a small and beautiful town located two and a half hours from Mexico City, where the Discalced Carmelite friars live and hold retreats of silence, prayer, and contemplation, following the spirituality of the great Carmelite saints and mystics. I then wanted to know the place and decided to participate in one of those retreats with the theme: "Life and Spirituality of Saint Theresa of Avila" led by *Father Miguel Angel Pérez Alonso, OCD,* the superior of the house and creator of such an incomparable place.

I must truthfully say that the first retreat I attended at *"Carmel Maranatha",* was a transforming spiritual experience that marked a turning point in my life. There I discovered the life and spirituality of **Saint Teresa of Avila, also know as Saint Teresa of Jesus, the founder of the Discalced Carmelites**, whom from that moment I embraced inwardly as my spiritual guide, and my new and great friend.

It was impressive how I felt in my soul that Saint Teresa was calling me to know her, to enter her life, her writings, her doctrine, and her spiritual path. This was a great gift because I felt that the initiative came personally from her to me, so I was deeply excited, wishing to get to know her better through my frequent participation in the retreats at *"Carmel Maranatha"*.

Carmel Maranatha House of Prayer

My first encounter with Father Miguel Angel was also another great gift, as I felt warmly welcomed by him and the other conventual Carmelite friars who opened the doors of the house to me as if it were my own home.

The multiple talents and teachings of Father Miguel Angel began to reveal to me the work that the Holy Spirit was doing in him in an extraordinary way. His creativity and his true passion were showing a different, beautiful, and seductive image of God, which, while immensely attractive for the external beauty of the place, made that beauty an unparalleled gateway to **discover the beauty of God,** printed in the soul of every human being by the infinite love of his Creator.

The tireless work of Father Miguel Angel made the House of Prayer a privileged place where visitors from the town of Valle de Bravo, tourists from many countries in the world came to visit, and those who participated in the retreats were amazed by the spirit and beauty of the place.

Beauty: a reflection of God´s glory

The spirit and beauty of *"Carmel Maranatha"*, manifested in its lovely spaces, unique architecture, the art and symbolism of its paintings, the beauty of its gardens, the welcoming silence of its sacred precincts, the murmur of its fountains, and the music prepared by Father Miguel Angel, all welcomed visitors from their arrival.

In short, everything that he created as a true architect of the Spirit, made *"Carmel Maranatha"* a house of prayer, unique, worth visiting, and above all, a place of retreats, where **every celebration, was immerse in its content and beauty,** touching the lives of the attendees, enamoring our hearts, and bringing to the life of those of us who arrived thirsty to drink from the sources of the Carmelite mystics, **a new awareness and an increased interest in the Carmelite spirituality.**

No doubt that **the beauty of "Carmel Maranatha" has been an incomparable means of discovering the love of God,** touching the lives of thousands of people who have entered that blessed place, and touched the radiance of God´s presence in the beautiful, the good, the true, and the divine.

For, as *Urs Von Balthasar*, the great theologian said:

> *"Beauty is the reflection of the glory of God in the world... the way in which love becomes visible."* [3]

Yes, **beauty being intuitive, directly captures the love of God, manifested in Christ Jesus, and carries us on the wings**

---
[3] Hans Urs Von Balthasar. Only Love is Credible. Ignatius Press. San Francisco. 2004. Preface.

of the Holy Spirit Who takes us directly into the mystery of divine love and its total abasement, as we read in the Scriptures:

For God so loved the world that he gave his one and only Son, that whoever believes in him shall not perish but have eternal life." (Jn 3:16)

From my first retreat at "Carmel Maranatha", many more followed. Over time, Father Miguel Angel invited me to give the retreats with him, and thus, I discovered with great joy and enormous surprise, the beautiful call that God was making to me to make those retreats a central part of my life.

The call and the answer

It was during a time of prayer that I experienced the call from God inviting me to dedicate myself to giving spiritual retreats. This call came as a surprise to me. I had never thought about becoming a retreat guide. However, I felt a deep sense of peace and joy in my heart as I considered this invitation.

After being confirmed in prayer of God´s will for me, **I said "yes" to the call,** as I perceived that in essence, it was Him, through Father Miguel Angel who was inviting me to participate in the beautiful mission of making Him intimately known, leading participants to discover His love through the great richness of Carmelite spirituality. This inspired me to teach them the practice of interior prayer, meditation, and contemplation, sharing with them the inspirations and teachings that I was receiving, which were transforming my life with the love of God, the Carmelite saints, his friends, and all those who participated in our retreats.

To date, I have given, lived, enjoyed, and shared many spiritual retreats with lots of people, both at Carmel Maranatha and at other retreat centers in Mexico and in Canada. Through them, I have witnessed how God has touched the hearts and lives of participants, encouraging them to live their faith with Him at the center of their lives, inviting them to know the life and work of His great friends, the saints, and to follow the path of human and spiritual growth towards fullness.

Three years ago, with the intrusion of the Coronavirus, the world turned upside down, and I had to stop giving retreats. As a result, I felt the need to search for new ways to give them through internet. This book is the result of that search, and in part, the transcription of a retreat I gave via Zoom on the spirituality of St. Thérèse of Lisieux.

Writing my retreats into books is a new project that moves me deeply, mainly as a gift and thanksgiving to God, who I sense wants me to do it, igniting in my heart the flame of His love to be kindled in others. For this reason, this project is also a gift to all those who have followed me, and to you, my reader, so that together with many others, we can contribute to inflame our suffering world with the light of Christ that shines beyond all darkness, as He promised:

For this is what the Lord has commanded us: "I have made you a light for the Gentiles, that you may bring salvation to the ends of the earth" (Acts 13:47)

PART ONE

"Spirit of God, fill my life"

Let's start by praying to the Holy Spirit.

Whenever I go on a retreat, I like to begin by asking the Holy Spirit to come to us, to illuminate us with His light, and to be among us, so that we can begin this adventure with Him.

Now, I invite you to follow the internet link, or to scan the QR that I give you, down below. Once you have it ready, sit comfortably, making sure your back is straight, then, close your eyes, and take three deep breaths. When you are calm, listen with a prayerful attitude to the melody and words of the video that I recommend below.

Ask the Holy Spirit to come to your heart and fill your entire being with His love at this moment. Let Him be the "pure water" that cleanses what is dirty, nourishes you with His gifts, heals your wounds, and beautifies and sanctifies yourself, body, mind, heart, and spirit. In silence, repeat the words of the song that I give to you.

Holy Spirit, Come to Us"

https://tinyurl.com/3nhx3v5n

Holy Spirit come to me.

Kindle in me the fire of your Love

The Eclipse of God in Modern World

From difficulty in struggle arise humility, brokenness of heart, gentleness, and sweetness.

When I began to prepare this retreat, the first thing that came to my mind was the darkness that we have been enduring for the past three years due to the appearance of the Coronavirus and its variants.

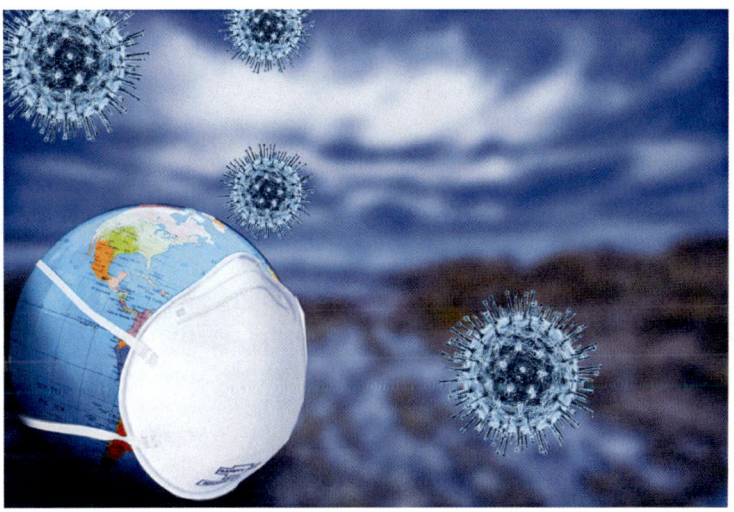

This virus, which surprised the entire world when we least expected it, has turned our lives upside down, **generating serious harm on a global scale and changing our way of living,** our relationships, our economic situation, and causing many people to suddenly finding themselves in extreme situations, feeling confused and insecure, and having great difficulty to manage emotions such as fear, anguish, anxiety, anger, and thoughts that have caused depression in many people, weakening their faith, hope and trust in God.

It is not surprising that sometimes, in the face of events like this, when we face great suffering, it is difficult to maintain our trust in God. **Jesus himself on the Cross experienced in His humanity a terrible sense of being abandoned by His Father.** His faith, hope, and love were tested to the limit until His death, but **despite all the outrages and sufferings He endured, never lost His trust in God,** for He knew that **God´s love is beyond all conflict and evil.**

Therefore, given the complex circumstances we are currently experiencing, it seems very important to touch in this book the topic of **trust and love of God, which are central to the spirituality of Saint Thérèse.**

I have no doubt that beyond any conflict, however terrible may seem, God is above them all and **wants us to face the challenges that arise with the certainty of His powerful love.** With Him, we can bring much good out of them, a good that will certainly surpass all the evils that afflict us today. Yes, we cannot forget that the power of God is not simply a human power; it is not a physical force or a mental force, no matter how challenging they may be. **The strength and power of God are manifested in our weakness, as Jesus said to St. Paul:** *"My grace is sufficient for you, for my power is made perfect in weakness."* Therefore, St. Paul could answer: *"I will rather boast most gladly of my weaknesses, in order that the power of Christ may dwell with me."* (2 Cor.12: 9)

The events that currently afflicting us are very serious. Just a few months ago, we were hopeful when we saw how Covid-19 and its variants were losing strength; however, we had not even gotten out of this, when the war between Ukraine and Russia broke out. This event left us perplexed, questioning what lies ahead. This war is leaving thousands, and thousands of dead and wounded, an immense number of people who have had to leave their homes and their countries, who lost all their belongings, family, and friends, and who have been forced to seek refuge in countries that allowed them to enter to safeguard their lives. A horror in which violence and thirst for power are once again affecting not only Ukraine and Russia, but the whole world.

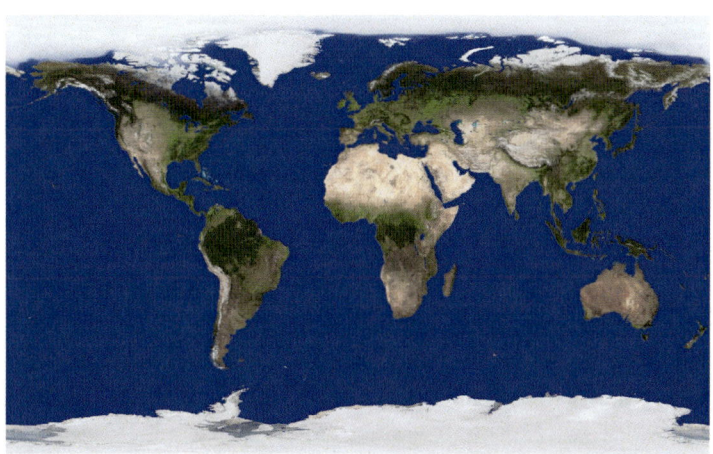

On the other hand, **we are witnessing how global warming is increasingly affecting our entire planet**. Many places are suffering from enormous droughts, in which the lack of rain is destroying fauna and vegetation, in addition to causing serious fires that force the inhabitants of those places to flee, leaving everything behind to stay alive. I invite you to take a break and watch: **The Pope, the Environmental Crisis, and Frontline Leaders | The Letter: Laudato Si Film.**

https://tinyurl.com/yb2y5jay

In contrast to the drought, we also see how terrible floods are occurring in other parts of the world, sweeping away entire villages, and forcing the residents to flee desperately in search of safety.

We have just been deeply shocked and saddened by the terrible earthquakes that certain cities in Turkey and Syria have suffered. We see with great pain the images that come to us through television of buildings collapsing as if they were made from paper, and in which many people have been buried under the rubble, leaving behind in mourning not only Ukraine and Russia, but the entire world.

These natural phenomena that we are experiencing today are also joined by the darkness of the current world, which is not only suffering from the violence of war, threats against the life of the planet, and the harmful effects of nature in response to the abuses we are causing it. In addition, **we are witnessing the increasingly greater deterioration in the perception of the nature and dignity of human life.** Above all of this, there are attacks and persecutions against believers, wanting to remove God from human life by continuously promoting contempt and rejection of His commandments. **Sadly, we are seeing laws and proposals that border on the absurd being accepted by governments, where everyone decides what is right and wrong, regardless of the consequences.**

"My people have committed two sins: They have forsaken me, the spring of living water, and have dug their own cisterns.
(Jer 2:13)

St. John Paul II, in his Encyclical *"The Gospel of Life,"* warned us about this, telling us how **the conscience of humanity has become sick and no longer knows how to distinguish between good and evil.** He said...*"When the sense of God is lost, the sense of man is also threatened and contaminated."* The Second Vatican Council affirmed the same: "The creature without the

Creator disappears...Moreover, by forgetting God, the creature itself becomes obscure."[4]

Faced with such a harsh reality that is increasingly affecting humanity, we need to become aware of the gravity of the situation in the world today and **pray for a global conversion** that leads us to face the challenges being truly responsible to stop the great threats that are endangering the life of our planet, our own lives, and that of future generations.

In a society where everything is valued in economic benefit, acquisition of social prestige, and political power, and where everything else is postponed as useless, **Christianity must proclaim**, as Hans Urs Von Balthasar did, that...

> *"Only Love is worthy of faith... The only reward for love is love itself. Good works must be an echo of love. Otherwise, they are worthless.*[5]

At the beginning of this spiritual retreat, I mentioned the importance of going to drink from the fountain of living water, which is Jesus.

In the Gospel there is a story that tells us about the Samaritan woman when she arrives at the well to draw water and meets Jesus comes to mind. He takes the initiative and says to her, "Woman, give me a drink." She is surprised and replies, "How can you, a Jew, ask me, a Samaritan woman, for a drink?" (Jews and Samaritans did not associate with each other). Jesus responds to her, "If you knew the gift of God and who it is that asks you for a drink, you would have asked him, and he would have given

---

[4] en.wikipedia.org › wiki › Evangelium_Vitae
[5] Hans Urs Von Balthasar. Only Love is Credible. Ignatius Press. San Francisco. 2004. Preface.

you living water... Whoever drinks the water I give them will never thirst. Indeed, the water I give them will become in them a spring of water welling up to eternal life." (Jn 4: 7-14)

Water is the indispensable element for life. Anselm Grün, a Benedictine monk and great writer, tells in his book *"Sources of Inner Strength"* how years ago, when the monks of the Münsterchwarzach Abbey in Germany, where he lives, were renovating it and needed water, they dug a well and found it about five meters deep, but as **it was a relatively shallow depth,** the water seeped through and stopped flowing when it was hot. Furthermore, that water was not pure but cloudy. **To solve the problem, the monks had to dig deeper until they found groundwater that would not seep through or run out.**

How often do we settle for staying in superficial and cloudy waters that, although they apparently quench our thirst, end up making us sick? Let us not settle for drinking from those waters but **let us go deeper to find pure and vital water of the Holy**

Spirit, which truly refreshes us and changes what is turbid within us into pure and delicious water. **Let us go to the source from which that new life-giving water flows** so that we can truly renew our lives, heal ourselves inwardly and outwardly, **and offer them to others as St. Therese did.** Let us turn to the Virgin Mary and ask her, as our Mother, to **teach us to differentiate between the types of water we drink.** I think of the water of Lourdes and the apparitions of the Blessed Virgin to Bernadette in the Grotto of Massabielle, where the spring of water has cured multitude of people.

There is no doubt that today more than ever we need to go beyond all the chaos and turmoil of the world, looking beyond, without forgetting that **we have been justified by faith, we are at peace with God through our Lord Jesus Christ;** it is through him, by faith, that we have been admitted into God's favour in which we are living, and look forward exultantly to God's glory. Not only that; let us exult, too, in our hardships, understanding that **hardship develops perseverance, and perseverance develops a tested character, something that gives us hope,** and a hope which will not let us down, because as we read in the Scriptures:

"The love of God has been poured into our hearts by the Holy Spirit which has been given to us. (Rom 5:1-5)

We see that despite all the evil in the world, the many threats against human life, the ideologies wanting to remove God from our lives, wars, destructive natural phenomena, and the chaos we have been experiencing as a result of the appearance of Covid-19, this tiny virus has not been able to reign or end humanity, but has awakened the consciousness of many people who have faced it with enormous courage, immediately seeking solutions to overcome it. It is not in vain that the saying goes: *"every cloud has a silver lining"*.

Hope for the world

During these grave threats, we have witnessed how Covid-19 and its variants **have raised among us many heroes and heroines** who, with their commitment to addressing the urgent needs of humanity, and their tireless work, have become true examples of goodness and solidarity.

Since the beginning of the pandemic, we have witnessed a multitude of doctors, nurses, and hospital staff who have saved thousands and thousands of lives, even putting their own lives at risk. I remember with great emotion what I experienced in Vancouver during the time of the highest contagion. Every evening, at exactly 6:00 pm, the city's population would unite from their homes going out onto their balconies and patios, making noise with pots, pans, and bells as a sign of our gratitude to all the medical personnel who were tirelessly attending to the sick, regardless of their fatigue and risking their lives. It was impressive to witness the solidarity that was shown throughout the city and not only there, but in many parts of the world.

Thanks to the creativity and tireless work of the staff in supermarkets, pharmacies, clinics, and other service establishments, we could obtain the products needed without having to physically go out to get them. Suddenly, schools and universities began to develop online programs so that students could continue their studies. On the other hand, priests started to become experts in Zoom, Facebook, YouTube, and other social networks, so that we could participate daily in Masses and different evangelization programs. All kinds of support were produced at breakneck speed to face the global crisis as best as possible.

Something fantastic was to see how researchers from different parts of the world moved with enormous speed trying to develop vaccines that could prevent further contagion, and much earlier than expected, they managed to produce the long-awaited vaccines, and immediately, several pharmaceutical companies began to manufacture and distribute them in all continents.

Having to remain confined in our homes, current technology was the best weapon to help companies continue working, to ensure that workers did not lose their jobs and could continue doing their work from home.

At the international level, there was great collaboration that has succeeded, after three years, in greatly reducing contagion and the risk of death. Thanks to all of this, we have been able to gradually emerge from our confinement and recover some tranquility.

The work of each individual working as a team has been impressively efficient, and **it shows how we can bring out the goodness that exists in the human heart and soul, which arises from our very essence, reminding us that God created us in His image and likeness.**

We have been witnessing how from this divine origin, good, love, light, and brotherhood can emerge among us when we unite as brothers to face and overcome the threats of evil.

At this point, I think about Viktor E. Frankl[6], the great Viennese neuropsychiatrist, who was imprisoned and sent to the concentration camp during World War II.

He recounts in his book *"Man's Search for Meaning"* a double reality. On the one hand, the cruelty of many of the Nazi guards in the concentration camp who delighted in torturing the prisoners, but he also explains how among them, there were guards who showed kindness towards the prisoners.

On the other hand, he talks about how among the prisoners themselves there were some of extraordinary kindness, willing to give their only piece of bread to a sick person who was dying of hunger, but also how there were others who were as cruel as the Nazi guards themselves. It is a reality that, in the moments of greatest trials, of great conflicts, we have the freedom to choose what kind of people we want to be.

Right now, we are witnessing the enormous global solidarity to aid the victims of earthquakes in Turkey and Syria. It is touching to see on television the images of thousands of people from different countries around the world rescuing day and night multitude of people who have been trapped under the rubble.

It becomes evident that disasters bring out the best in people, and amid so much evil and darkness the light and love of God emerge to remind us that the imprint of His love exists in every human being. A love that surpasses all evil, manifested in so

---

[6] https://en.wikipedia.org/wiki/Viktor E. Frankl

many people willing to give their lives for others and to fill us with hope during times of chaos, remembering what Jesus said:

"Do not fear, for I am with you; Do not be dismayed, for I am your God. I will strengthen you; I will surely help you, Yes, I will uphold you with My righteous right hand." (Isaiah 41:10)

Jesus makes an urgent call to us to become aware of the current reality and not fall into the chaos of the culture of death, but rather to fight for the culture of life to penetrate all environments of society.

This makes me think of a recent homily given by Father Richard Conlin during Mass at Corpus Christi Church in Vancouver, when he told us how in the Arizona desert, vultures and hummingbirds live in the same harsh environment, but their way of life is radically different.

Vultures only seek what is dead; they are on the lookout for rotting meat and do not stop until they find animal carcasses to feed on, and if they cannot find them, they look for live animals to kill and eat. Vultures are birds of prey.

On the other hand, hummingbirds are very small birds with beautiful colors, wings that fly at great speeds, and a long beak that allows them to drink the nectar of flowers, which they use as their source of food while also aiding in the pollination of plants by distributing their flower pollen from flower to flower.

These small birds seek what is alive, beautiful, and generate life for themselves and their surroundings; vultures do not. Father Richard asked us: Which of these birds are we called to imitate?

We are not called to be vultures but hummingbirds.

We are called not to fall into despair but to confront evil by doing good, taking care of ourselves and others, being bearers of the delicious nectar of God's love, and being in solidarity with each other so that we do not become infected by evil but instead help developing a true Christian culture of life that grows good in our own lives, in the lives of others, and in the life of God in the world.

As you are reading this, something very beautiful is happening, and that is precisely that Jesus is calling you and saying...

"I am the gate; whoever enters through me will be saved."
(Jn10:9)

Yes, today, in a special way, Jesus is calling you personally, he wants to visit you in your situation, he wants to be with you in the challenges you are facing, in your struggles, in your dreams, and in the whatever situation that arise. **Jesus wants to give you** His strength, the light of faith, the breath of hope, and the incomparable joy of knowing He is always faithful, and present to help you go through all difficulties, no matter how terrible they may seem, and **He wants to do this through Saint Thérèse.**

St. Thérèse: Your great spiritual teacher

When I prepare a talk, a course, or a retreat, beautiful inspirations come to me thinking about **the work that the Lord wants to accomplish in each participant, and generally these inspirations come accompanied by the saints, His friends**.

In this spiritual spa, I have felt deeply in my heart that St. Thérèse of the Child Jesus, doctor of the Church, wants to be present, wants to accompany you, wants to share her teachings with you. She wants to be with you and talk to you about her great discovery, which we know as the **"little way of spiritual childhood"** which is a path of trust, and abandonment in God´s unsurmountable love, in which we can rely, like that of a child who knows he is loved and trusting falls asleep without fear in the arms of his father..."

That "little way" is a simple path that both you, me and everyone can follow to reach holiness. Saint Thérèse followed that path and therefore, is the perfect teacher to let you know how to face the various circumstances of your life following the way that led her to become not only one of the greatest saints of our time, but also be proclaimed doctor of the Church by Pope St. John Paul II on October 19, 1997, in St. Peter's Basilica in Rome, on the centenary of her death.

Before continuing, it seems important to clarify, in case you didn't know, that **St. Thérèse of the Child Jesus,** also known as the **Little Flower,** or **St. Thérèse of Lisieux**, by the name of the city where she lived in France, is not the same as **St. Teresa of Jesus**, also known as **St. Teresa of Avila**, by the place where she lived in Spain, and who **was the founder of the Discalced Carmelites in the sixteenth century.** Instead, St. Thérèse was born in the **nineteenth century, in Alençon, France,** and later lived in Lisieux, France. She became a Discalced Carmelite; therefore, **she is a spiritual daughter of St. Teresa of Jesus or of Avila.** It is important to make this distinction because there are several saints with the name Teresa, such as **St. Theresa of Calcutta, St. Theresa of the Andes, St. Theresa Benedicta of the Cross, and others.** Therefore, it can be very confusing, but once this clarification is made, let us continue with St. Thérèse of the Child Jesus.

In these pages, I want to reflect with you on **key aspects of her spiritual journey,** with the **main purpose that you reflect on your own life and recognize the unique work that God has been doing in you all through the years**.

It is very important, that you know with certainty how God has been present and continues always to be present in your life without you even realizing it. **In your reflections you will discover this, as well as His will for you today through the spirituality of St. Thérèse.**

The battle we are currently facing in the world is not only a battle at human level, but also and **mainly a battle at spiritual level.** Therefore, **Jesus wants to give you His Spirit**, so that His Spirit may unite with your spirit and testify that you are a son, a daughter of God. Yes, because **the Holy Spirit is the one who cares for our identity as children of God,** who purifies, illuminates, and sanctifies us.

The Holy Spirit is also the One who teaches us to pray and **introduces us to a true relationship of friendship and love with God,** teaching us to believe, trust, hope, and love, as He did with St. Thérèse.

All that is precisely what He wants to do with you. in this very moment of your life.

Are you ready to let Him, do it?

****

Some Data of St. Thérèse

Marie-Françoise Thérèse Martin Guerin[7] was born on a Thursday, January 2, 1873, in Alençon, a small city of the province of Normandy in northern France.

Thérèse, was the last daughter of Zélie Guérin and Louis Martin, who had nine children, four of whom died at a young age, and

---

[7] https://en.wikipedia.org/wiki/Thérèse_of_ Lisieux

only five girls survived. Marie the oldest, Pauline, Léonie, Céline, and Thérèse, who was the last.

Saint Thérèse´s Family

Louis Martin (22 August 1823 – 29 July 1894) Zélie Guérin (23 December 1831 – 28 August 1877). Married on July 13,1858 and had nine children. They were canonized October 18, 2015

<u>Marie Louise</u> (22 February 1860 – 19 January 1940), as a nun, *Sister Marie of the Sacred Heart*, Carmelite at Lisieux.

Marie Pauline (7 September 1861 – 28 July 1951), as a nun, *Mother Agnès of Jesus*, Carmelite at Lisieux.

Marie Léonie (3 June 1863 – 16 June 1941), as a nun, *Sister Françoise-Thérèse*, Visitandine at Caen; candidate for sainthood since January 2015.

Marie Hélène (3 October 1864 – 22 February 1870).

Joseph Louis (20 September 1866 – 14 February 1867).

Joseph Jean-Baptiste (19 December 1867 – 24 August 1868).

Marie Céline (28 April 1869 – 25 February 1959), as a nun, *Sister Geneviève of the most Holy Face*, Carmelite at Lisieux.

Marie Melanie-Thérèse (16 August 1870 – 8 October 1870)

Marie Françoise-Thérèse (2 January 1873 – 30 September 1897), as a nun, *Sister Thérèse of the Child Jesus and of the Holy Face*, Carmelite at Lisieux, canonised in 1925, Doctor of the Church, 1997.

****

Her life on earth begins

Few days after she was born, her health was threatened by enteritis, an inflammation of her intestine. Her mother could not nurse her, so **she had to be nursed** by **Rose Taillé**, who lived in Semaillé, a little town in the countryside, about fifteen kilometers from Alençon.

When she was fifteen months old, Thérèse returned to her family life and was surrounded by the love of her parents and sisters. However, this happiness did not last long, as when she was only four years old, she had to face the painful loss of her mother, who died of breast cancer.

The loss of her mother caused in her a terrible tear, which was later joined by other painful losses, when three of her sisters went to the convent, one after the other.

All these sufferings caused her serious instability, manifested in **physical and emotional fragility,** which kept her from living a normal life until she was ten years old due to a rare illness that made her live terrible scruples in her soul, making her see evil and sin where there was none. This caused her to continuously analyze her conscience making her doubt continuously, as all the options she found seemed useless and kept her in a permanent state of anguish.

The Virgin´s smile

It was at that age, on May 13th, 1883, while sick in her bed, that she suddenly saw the image of the Blessed Virgin Mary that was placed in her bedroom, smiling at her. The Virgin's smile made her feel very much loved and accompanied to such an extent, **that the Virgin's smile restored her physical health.**[8]

---

[8] Story of a Soul. ICS Publications. Washington D.C. Third Edition p. 65

However, although she was cured of her physical illness, she still had to spend four more years of great struggles with her terrible scruples before being deeply healed emotionally. It was on December 25, 1886, when she received a new grace, that she calls **"the grace of Christmas."** In this grace, she not only regained her emotional stability but also took a great leap towards maturity.

She tells us: "It was necessary for God to do a little miracle to make me grow in a moment, and that miracle was done on the unforgettable day of Christmas. On that luminous night that clarifies the delights of the Holy Trinity, Jesus, the sweet newborn baby, changed the night of my soul into torrents of light... on that night, in which he became weak and suffering for my love, he made me strong and courageous; **he clothed me with his weapons, and from that blessed night on, I knew**

no defeat in any battle, but on the contrary, **I went from victory to victory and began, so to speak, a race of giants."**[9]

The grace that Saint Thérèse received on Christmas can also be requested by us. **The grace of coming out of our fears and insecurities** by living the season of Advent as a joyful anticipation of the birth of Jesus at Christmas, and thus become instrument of the Holy Spirit. **Let us live that season of the year focussing our attention and actions on Jesus, not on material things, or shopping.**

Let us ask the Blessed Virgin that the grace of Christmas comes true in us so that we may bring about **a change of mentality not only in ourselves but in our environment,** for we see with great concern how there is an increasing demand to even remove the name of "Merry Christmas" in favor of "Happy Holidays", forgetting in this way **the essential and truly central aspect of Christmas which is the birth of Jesus coming into the world as our Redeemer.**

Returning to the subject of the grace that Thérèse received at Christmas which changed her life, she tells us how **since she was a little girl, she had desired to become a nun and enter the Carmelite convent in the city of Lisieux.**

Her fervent desire became a reality when, through the work and grace of God, **she was accepted at the age of fifteen as a postulant in the convent.** She lived there for only nine years, as she fell ill with tuberculosis and **died because of this fatal illness at the age of twenty-four on September 30, 1897.** After her death, as was customary, the Carmelite nuns, published a posthumous note about her along with her autobiography, which

---

[9] Story of a Soul. ICS Publications. Washington D.C. Third Edition p. 97

unexpectedly soon became a highly successful book called: **"Story of a Soul."**[10]

Its publication quickly spread around the world, touching the hearts of many people. The extraordinary number of favors received from Saint Thérèse by those who invoked her intercession, also contributed to her fame. When one visits the church attached to the Carmelite convent in the city of Lisieux, **it is impressive to see all the walls covered with plaques thanking her for the thousands of miracles and favors received**.

Story of a Soul

Her book, *"Story of a Soul",* has become a **key reference for understanding and practicing the message of the Gospel in the circumstances of the current world,** as it contains the

---

[10] Story of a Soul. ICS Publications. Washington D.C. Third Edition Introduction

force of truth, as **Pope Saint John Paul II** said in his homily on the day, he named her the youngest **doctor of the Church**:

"She helps us rediscover the heart of the Gospel: the tenderness of God the Father and the path of spiritual childhood by which we are called to become little children in the eyes of God" [11]

In the Gospel, we find many words of Jesus on this subject when he said:

"Unless you change and become like little children, you will never enter the kingdom of heaven" (Mt 18:3).

Let us remember how, on one occasion, when Jesus' disciples were arguing about who among them would be the greatest in the kingdom of heaven, Jesus placed a child among them and said:

"Whoever welcomes this little child in my name welcomes me, and whoever welcomes me welcomes the one who sent me. For it is the one who is least among you all who is the greatest" (Lk 9:48).

Psychology of Caresses

Each of us has the need to live that inner transformation that makes us as small as children. This means that we must put into practice what Saint Thérèse tells us in a simple and luminous way through her **little way of trust and love.**

Eric Berne [12] creator of Transactional Analysis, talks about the **"psychology of caresses"**, and of the **importance to know**

---

[11] John Paul II, Vatican VA. Proclamation of St. Thérèse of the Child Jesus and the Holy Face as a "Doctor of the Church" 19-10-97

[12] https:// en.wikipedia.org. Eric Berne

our inner child. He calls **"caress"** to any act that involves recognition of the presence of another. Caresses are an essential form of emotional communication when we try to convey our affection to someone else.

These caresses become stimuli that **act in our lives from the beginning and affect us positively or negatively.** Just as we need to eat to survive from birth, we also need caresses that make us be recognized by others and grow mentally, emotionally, and spiritually healthy.

Eric Berne says that **the caresses we receive during our childhood** are the ones that organize what he calls our **"life script"**, which **shapes our personality**. It is like the inherited script **in which the person plays a certain role that leads him or her to act according to the character each represent**.

In the early years of our life, a script is established under the influence of our parents and other influential people. **This script is reinforced according to what we experience**, and it can confirm the script received from others and the environment, making it more important than our own experience. However, **we can modify this "inherited" script later**, when we become aware of the elements that have conditioned us and then **decide to change them to aspire to a fuller and more authentic life.**

It is interesting to see how **the circumstances in which we are conceived and born can affect our life script.** In the case of **Saint Thérèse,** we can recall that she was the last of nine children and was born after four of her siblings had died. This was very painful for her parents, sisters, and family, and it certainly had an impact on the script that Thérèse lived, as **she had to fight for her health from the beginning of her life.**

At two weeks old, she was on the brink of death because of neonatal enteritis. Neonatal enteritis is an inflammation of the small intestine that can be caused by a variety of factos, incluing infection and poor nutrition.

As I mentioned earlier, her mother couldn´t nurse her. **To survive,** Thérèse had to be cared for **by Rose Taillé,** her wet nurse who lived about fifteen kilometers away from Thérèse´s family´s home in Alençon. This meant that **Thérèse was away from her family during the first year of her life** becoming accustomed to living in the countryside with Rose and her family.

At the end of that time, she left Semaillé, separated from Rose Taillé and return to her family's home.

For the next three years, she was cared for and much loved by her mother, her father, and her four sisters; but, then **at the age of four, she suffered the terrible loss of her mother´s death.** After her mother´s passing, Thérèse took her sister **Pauline as her "second mother"**, feeling protected and much loved by her, but when she was eight years old, she received the sad news that Pauline would leave her to go to the convent.

Because of all these separations since she was born, first from her mother, then from Rose, later from Pauline, and soon after that, from Marie and Léonie, who also entered the convent, we see how **her early life and childhood were marked by profound feelings of losses and sense of abandonment,** which greatly influenced the development of her personality, or as Eric Berne would say, **the "script" of her life.**

In this regard, it can be interesting to question ourselves about **our own lives,** to see **how the internal and external events** of our family, our cultural, social, and religious environment **influenced our early years and marked certain patterns that affected our personality, behavior, and life script.**

Returning to the topic of "caresses," *Eric Berne* says that **if we receive positive caresses in our childhood,** we will surely be well nourished internally and will easily connect with our original dignity. **In contrast, if we receive negative caresses**, **our self-esteem and identity could be damaged** and may affect our perception of the world, ourselves, our relationships, and the image we have of God.

In some way, **we have all have received both positive and negative caresses,** some more than others. As we have seen, **Saint Thérèse also had to be physically and psychologically healed from her physical, emotional and abandonment wounds,** but after struggling for fourteen years, she finally learned to take advantage of the many positive caresses she received from her father, sisters, uncles, and some of her community in the convent, but **above all, what healed her was the love of God** who filled her with grace and wisdom. No wonder that at becoming aware of all she lived, she will later say: **"All is grace."**

Like Saint Thérèse, **it can be very enlightening for us to recognize the kind of caresses we have received at human level, but especially the caresses we have received from God.** Therefore, in this retreat, **I encourage you to undertake that inner search to discover the caresses** that have contributed positively, and those that have affected your human and spiritual development in some way.

Saint Thérèse openly shares what she herself had to endure before she could be healed, and not only that, but also **how she learned to change the negative caresses into positive ones,** based on the grace and love of Jesus and the healing action of the Virgin Mary and of the Holy Spirit.

I suggest that you take some time to **reflect on this topic and go through the stages of your life,** invoking the Virgin of the Smile, and the Holy Spirit, **to help you heal what still hurts you, and to discover and nurture what has helped you move forward until today.** Answering the questions, I give you will guide you to reflect on the script of your life in your early years and how it has unconsciously influenced you. While you review those early stages of your life. I join you spiritually in prayer.

Questions for your reflection:

* What script do you think Thérèse had to play in her childhood?

* What helped her to heal?

* What script have you played in your family?

* According to that script, what kind of person are you supposed to be?

* Do you feel fine with that script, or would you like to change it?

* What script do you play among your friends?

* What script do you have socially?

* According to those scripts, how are you supposed to do in your life?

* How can you do to change what you don't like about your early script?

This reminds me of how we must get new spiritual clothes when the old one's don´t fit any more.

The process of human and spiritual healing takes time and requires a lot of patience. We need to trust and be sure that when we ask Jesus, Our Lady, the Holy Spirit, and St. Thérèse to heal our wounds, and we do our part, they will also do their part in due time. **All the events in our lives are means to heal, grow, and mature**, just as they were for Saint Thérèse, who struggled to free herself from what made her have a negatively image of herself, often living sunk in a dark hole that prevented her from seeing the light.

When we are sunk in a dark hole, **we can also be as children, asking Jesus to come into our lives, to take us in His arms and lift us up** so that, from His height, we can contemplate another reality; a reality that fills us with confidence in His love, and **allows us to surrender ourselves to Him**, knowing that nothing and no one can separate us from the immense joy of knowing ourselves as children of God unconditionally and eternally loved.

We read in the Gospel:

What will separate us from the love of Christ? Will anguish, or distress, or persecution, or famine, or nakedness, or peril, or the sword? No, in all these things we conquer overwhelmingly through him who loved us. For I am convinced that neither death, nor life, nor angels, nor principalities, nor present things, nor future things, nor powers, nor height, nor depth, nor any other creature will be able to separate us from the love of God in Christ Jesus our Lord (Romans 8:35, 37-39).

The Little Way of Spiritual Childhood

"I feel that my mission is about to begin, the mission to make people love God as I love Him, to teach my little way to souls. The way of spiritual childhood, of trust and total abandonment." [13]

---

[13] Last Conversations, July 17, 1897

In this retreat, I want us to pay special attention to the **"little way of spiritual childhood"**, which, as St. Thérèse says, is for everyone, as it is a very simple and direct path that we can follow in our daily lives. This will help us discover more about **the good news of the Gospel**, as it is always **good news**, and not a law that crushes us.

Yes, dear reader, **the Gospel must always be understood as joyful news to fill our hearts with love, consolation, hope, and peace.**

While it is true that Jesus' teachings are demanding at times, Thérèse helps us see them as true good news, since, as she says, the Gospel is nothing less than the revelation of God's tender and merciful love for his children because,

> *"God so loved the world that he gave his only Son, so that everyone who believes in him might not perish but might have eternal life." (Jn 3:16)*

The Gospels: God's love letters

I invite you to **always read the Gospels as love letters**, not as if they were math textbooks, where two plus two equals four and that's it. No, a love letter is read between the lines; it invites us to think about what the person who wrote it meant, to question his or her words, and even try to imagine what he or she meant beyond the lines.

A love letter touches and penetrates our heart; it is savored, smelled, kissed, read, and reread countless times. It is reflected upon, felt, and kept in a very special place. A love letter moves us inside, makes us fall in love and feel most joyful, as it reaffirms the fact that we are valuable, and loved by the sender is a very special way.

64

A love letter moves us inside to respond to the one who sent it with the same love, and even makes us desire to surpass that love to correspond with more love. **The Gospels are letters of God's Love for us, where Jesus´s life, shows us the magnitude of His immense, incomparable, and eternal Love.**

We must always remember that **the central core, the heart of Christian life is Love**, therefore, receiving, and welcoming God's Love, His goodness, His tenderness, the revelation of His mercy, **prepares us to be inwardly transformed by Him**. He is Love Himself.

> *"So, we have come to know and to believe the love that God has for us. God is love, and whoever remains in love remains in God and God in him." (1 John 4:16)*

When Saint Thérèse described in ***"Story of a Soul"*** the little way of spiritual childhood, **she was aware of having a particularly deep and new perception of the Gospel.** She wanted to pass it on to the nuns who lived with her in the convent, especially to the novices, of whom she was their teacher. However, sharing that new vision of the Gospel remained very restricted for her during her life, and it was only after she died that her teachings have spread throughout the world in an extraordinary way.

Just before her death, she wrote:

"I desire to spend my heaven doing good on earth"[14]

and what she could not do in life, she has been doing since she went to heaven. Surely, she also wants to do it in you today, if you ask her to teach you **how to live her little way of spiritual childhood, and how to abandon yourself in God´s merciful love**, and learn to love Him, as she did: with all her soul, with all her heart, and with all her whole being.

What is the Little Way of Spiritual Childhood about?

The little way of spiritual childhood **is a path that takes away all fear, all doubt, all guilt, and reminds us that God loves us always and unconditionally.** It is a path that makes us surrender to God and fills us with confidence in His merciful love. **God accepts us just as we are despite our faults and forgives us whenever we ask for it.**

The little way of spiritual childhood is a path **accessible to all those who become like children; small and humble,** letting themselves be guided by God, knowing that He oversees our lives, so that no one becomes discouraged, not even the greatest sinners.

It is a path in which we follow God's desires, God's will, discovering His plan of love, and confidently surrendering to the

---

[14] Story of a Soul. ICS Publications. Washington D.C. Third Edition p..263

action of the Holy Spirit **as He helps us live the conversion of our heart.** The desire to follow Jesus' plan for us, **will finally conform us to His image and make us mature, happy, and saints.**

Our Desires

We all carry great desires in our souls. The word desire is used very often by mystics. **Desire is a force that sets us in motion internally.** It is a source that feeds our energy and makes us face **challenges with determination** working to overcome them and looking for ways **to bring our dreams to life.** That is why it is extremely important that you **discover what your desires are.**

All human beings, we, are people of desires, whether we know it or not. When we are not aware of our desires or lack them, our life becomes tedious, boring, depressing, and meaningless.

Nothing is achieved without great desires. We need to desire great and good things and act on those desires to bring them to life. **Desires require action, otherwise, they will remain frustrated within us.**

If we look at the world, at the valuable things that have emerged over the centuries, we see that **great and good desires are always the source from which best projects arise.**

Discoveries, great works, and enterprises have always been forged by men and women who wanted to fight with all their might to ensure that their desires become a reality. **We need two things: to desire great things, and to act.**

This reminds me of the story of *Ryan Hreljac* [15] a Canadian boy who, at the age of six, was in school when his teacher spoke to the class about many children in Africa who had to walk long distances to get a little bit of water.

The story of Ryan Hreljac

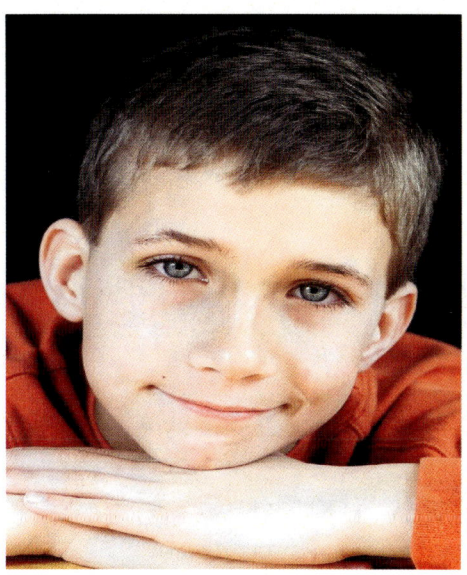

The water they found and drank even though it quenched their thirst was not safe to drink and caused many diseases. This moved Ryan so much that he desired to do something about it. He started to do some research and learned that there was a Canadian organization building wells in Africa. Motivated by his desire to help the children his teacher spoke about, he decided to raise enough money to build a well for those children.

---

[15] https://en.Wikipedia.org Ryan Hreljac

Ryan began asking for help from his parents, family, classmates, friends, then to the rest of the students and teachers in his school, after that, to others in nearby schools. **He continued asking for help everywhere** and **at the end of the year he had raised enough money to build his first well at the Angola Primary School in northern Uganda.**

Encouraged by the results, **he decided to continue working to build more wells, this leading to the creation of "Ryan's Well Foundation,"** through which he has been able to help build over 700 wells, providing access to safe drinking water for more than 700,000 people in about thirty countries in Africa, Asia, and Latin America.

In 2014, he graduated with a degree in International Development and Political Science from the University of Halifax. He currently travels around the world giving lectures on the importance of water as an essential element of life and fighting against the lack of access to water in poor countries. His work has been recognized by UNICEF, and he has received the "Order of Ontario," the province's highest honor.

Ryan says about himself:

"There is nothing special about me; it was this project that turned out to be something incredible."

Today, he continues to encourage children and adults **to have great dreams** like him and **to work hard to overcome obstacles with determination until they see their desires come true.** He says:

"My advice to anyone is that, in order to make positive change in the world, you need to find something you are passionate about and then you need to take steps to act."

In this Spiritual Spa, **God calls you to recognize your desires,** not to be afraid of being idealistic, and to desire great things, be passionate about what you desire, work towards making them come true, and striving to achieve them, knowing that with the grace of the Holy Spirit, your desires will become a force that will move you inside, and lead you overcome problems that may arise, even if they are as complex as Ryan's. Do not be afraid to desire great things, to propose solutions to current problems, and to fight with all your might to obtain them. That is what will make you a great builder of your own life and that of others.

Here is a link to a video of Ryan so that you can learn more about him.

https://www.ryanswell.ca/about-ryans-well/

Our limitations: opportunities for triumph

Another person who comes to mind is *Andrea Bocelli*.[16] When his mother was pregnant, the doctor warned her that the child would be born with a severe disability and recommended to have an abortion. Andrea's parents did not accept what the doctor proposed and decided to have the child. Indeed, Andrea was born with vision problems and was diagnosed with congenital glaucoma. Currently, he says that his mother's decision to continue with the pregnancy, has been a great inspiration for him to become a public opponent of abortion, and a great promotor

---

[16] https:// en.wikipedia.org Andrea Bocelli

of human life. When Andrea turned twelve years old, he received a strong blow to the head during a soccer game, causing him total blindness. However, he decided that this would not destroy his life or to block his desires to continue his studies. Later, he pursued a career in Law at the University of Pisa while also taking singing classes to develop the great voice that God had gifted him. As a result, he has become one of the world's best singers.

It's impressive to read his biography and learn about the many countries where he has performed, as well as the numerous awards, honors, and recognitions he has received for his great work in favor of art and peace, uplifting the spirits of those who listen and uniting people of all races, nationalities, and religions through his singing. Andrea Bocelli currently has a foundation called ABF (Andrea Bocelli's Foundation) in Lajatico, Italy, the place where he was born, and its purpose is to build a better world by helping the less privileged through actions of love. He has been an important inspiration for many people around the world, while also receiving the encouragement of all those who have seen and heard him, stating with his own family.

As one of the beautiful fruits of his personal life, he currently has the enormous joy of sharing his talent with his son Matteo, whom he has guided and supported in his career as a professional musician and singer. Together, father and son have formed a duet and produced videos that are traveling the world.

Today, I want to recommend a very beautiful video where Andrea Bocelli and his son Matteo sing together, a beautiful song in which you can also see beautiful images of their lives.

Fall on Me

https://tinyurl.com/bde6pvxm

In addition to the satisfaction of encouraging his son Matteo in his career as a musician and singer, and now singing with him, Andrea is also teaching Virginia, his young daughter, how to sing. They have started recording some videos and concerts together. In this second video, you will see the three of them singing together. You will also learn about all the good that Andrea Bocelli's foundation is benefiting many people around the world. It's a great project that speaks of how it is possible to make dreams come true and share with others the talents God has given.

https://www.youtube.com/watch?v=m3vv768qagU

If you still want to listen to another joyful song with Andrea and his children here, I send you another link:

https://www.youtube.com/watch?v=--8ULkzKa-o

After you have watched and savored the videos, take some time for silence, reflection, and prayer. Sit comfortably and answer the questions I give you, not as a task that you must perform, but as an opportunity to enter yourself and give them your own meaning.

I invite you to think about your deepest desires and to tell Jesus, Our Lord:

"Come, my Jesus, help me discover your desires for me, and give me the capacity and determination to make your desires for me become a beautiful reality."

After you finish your reflection, take some time to pray about the topic of this chapter, and the answers you have given to the questions; finally, depending on how you have decided to do your retreat, rest a while, letting the Holy Spirit do His work in you. After that, when you are ready continue reading and living deeply the second part of this Spiritual Spa.

Questions for your reflection

* What has touched your heart the most in this first part of this Spiritual Spa?

* What does the "Way of Spiritual Childhood" invite you to?

* What positive caresses have you received since birth and from whom?

* How have these positive caresses helped you in your life?

* What negative caresses have you received, and from whom?

* What negative caresses do you still need to heal?

* What does Saint Thérèse teach you about what she experienced in her childhood?

* What ideas arise in you about Ryan's life?

* What desires come to you after watching the videos of Andrea Bocelli and his children?

* What are your biggest desires in life?

* What difficulties are you finding in achieving your desires?

* How can you overcome these difficulties?

* What has moved you the most in life?

Time for prayer

Now I recommend that you take some time for silent meditation and prayer to be with Jesus. Let Him inspire you so that you discover, in the light of the Holy Spirit, greater meaning about what you have read, and about the answers to the questions.

I give you *Father Rafael Checa OCD*, prayer method of interior prayer, who proposes you a simple and practical way to develop the practice of silent, meditative, and contemplative prayer.

We need to learn to pray life and live prayer. Remember that who perseveres, reaches. So, be patient with yourself, take courage, and you will see that practicing these four steps recommended by Father Checa, they will become part of your life and great support for your inner prayer.

The Rhythm of Prayer [17]

Process of mental prayer

1st Step: Preparation

a) Remote preparation: -Live with the purpose of pleasing God -Preserve God's presence as much as possible during the day -Try to organize your own activities -Have a daily time to pray.

---

[17] https:// en.wikipedia.org Andrea Bocelli

b) At time of prayer: -Deep and slow breathing -Relaxation of the body -Mental concentration -Attitude of faith, hope, and love

2nd Step: Transition

a) Reading: of the Word of God, or of the daily event (all events, sorrows, difficulties, problems, everything can be the subject of our dialogue with God.

b) Meditation: -Thinking, reflecting, illuminating the mystery of God and your relationship with Him.

3rd Step: The core of prayer

a) Affectionate dialogue: -Personal exchange with God. Talk to God and listen to Him in moments of silence.

b) Loving attention to God -Intuition of faith and love. Initial contemplation: recollection -We must all reach this moment.

4th Step: Before ending the prayer

a) Promise: -Practical conclusion, from considering to acting, from intuition to changing attitude, from love to pleasing and enjoying God, from desire to purpose.

b) Request -My weakness before the project and my change of attitude leads me to humbly ask God for His grace.

c) Thanksgiving: -In front of this gift: -God who communicates -Who makes Himself known -Who lets Himself be treated as a friend -Who lets Himself be loved -Who becomes an object of union -Who fills you with His life -Who desires to love you...

NOTES: -There is a constant interaction between prayer and life; prayer drives us to live better. Life provides new content to our prayer and makes it more fruitful.

-Although the most important thing in prayer is attitude, formal prayer times should not be neglected. Without them, the prayer attitude ends up diluting.

St. John Paul II tells us: "Learn to know Christ and let yourself be known by Him! You already know that before beginning His public life, Jesus withdrew to pray for 40 days in the desert. Well, try to create a little silence in your life too so that you can think, reflect, and pray with greater fervor and make resolutions with greater determination. Today it is difficult to create zones of desert and silence because we are continually caught up in thousand occupations, in the noise of events, in the demands of the media, so that inner peace is in danger, and elevated thoughts that should characterize human existence are hindered. It's difficult, but important to know how to do it."[18]

Once you have read and understood what the Rhythm of Prayer consists of, try to keep its four steps in mind, prepare the topic you are going to meditate on, and follow the steps during your time of prayer. I give you the link to **"To Live of Love"**, the beautiful the poem of St. Thérèse. Read each paragraph slowly, stop where something gets your attention, meditate on it, and ask Saint Thérèse to inspire you to discover the meaning it has forto you.

https://tinyurl.com/bddub4nu

---

[18] John Paul II, Ed. Monte Carmelo. Revista Orar No. 4, p. 22.

After you have meditated it carefully and lovingly, prepare yourself to pray.

Down below I give you the link to listen to the music for your prayer time. Sit comfortably and start listening to it following the four steps of the Rhythm of Prayer.

Close your eyes, place your hands on your knees, your feet firmly on the ground, and start breathing slowly and deeply, inhaling, and exhaling..., every time you inhale relax a part of your body, imagining the Holy Spirit entering your body bringing it new life, and when you exhale, He removes from you what hurts you and is not from God. Start breathing in and straightening your back, to slowly relaxing it..., then relax your feet..., legs..., abdomen..., chest..., shoulders..., neck..., face..., and head... Set aside all concerns and stay in peace, in silence and stillness, so that you are present in the here and now, and can meet Jesus, who awaits you in the silence of your heart.

I recommend you half hour of silent prayer.

Music for your prayer time

https://tinyurl.com/26tbnj5b

****

SECOND PART

God does not ask of us something impossible [19]

Congratulations! You have completed the first part of your Spiritual Spa, and I am sure that you are already receiving the blessings of God's love, Saint Therese's wonderful teachings, and the intercession of Our Lady, and Saint Joseph.

Let's recap.

In the first part of this retreat, I spoke to you about:

* The complicated situation in today's world, and the great challenges we face.

* The importance of facing these challenges by trusting in God's love, according to what Saint Thérèse tells in her little way of spiritual childhood.

* I told you about Eric Berne and the Psychology of Caresses. What he says about the effect of positive and negative "caresses" in childhood and how they can shape our life's script.

* I talked to you about Saint Thérèse childhood. The looses she had to face since her birth that affected her, and the physical and emotional illness she had to endure.

* Mentioned how her autobiography *"Story of a Soul"*, became a best seller since its first publication soon after her death and encouraged you to read it to discover her attractive simplicity, wisdom, and delve deeper into her life and spirituality.

---

[19] Story of a Soul. ICS Publications. Washington D.C. Third edition p. 207

* Invited you to read the Gospels as Letters of God's loving care for you, that guide you to fully live according to His will.

* Emphasized the importance of our desires in life and shared with you the stories of Ryan Hreljac and Andrea Bocelli, to inspire you as to pursue your own desires and turn them into reality.

* Gave you questions to help you internalize on your experiences in the topics you have read.

* Explain to you Father Checa´s "Rhythm of Prayer", to use it as your prayer method.

* Gave you links and QR codes of St. Thérèse poem "To Live of Love".

* Recommended you the link and QR code to listen to instrumental music during your prayer time.

In this second part of your Spiritual Spa, I want to continue delving deeper with you into the significant topic of desires, but now in reference to Saint Thérèse's desires.

****

St. Thérèse, the saint of immense desires

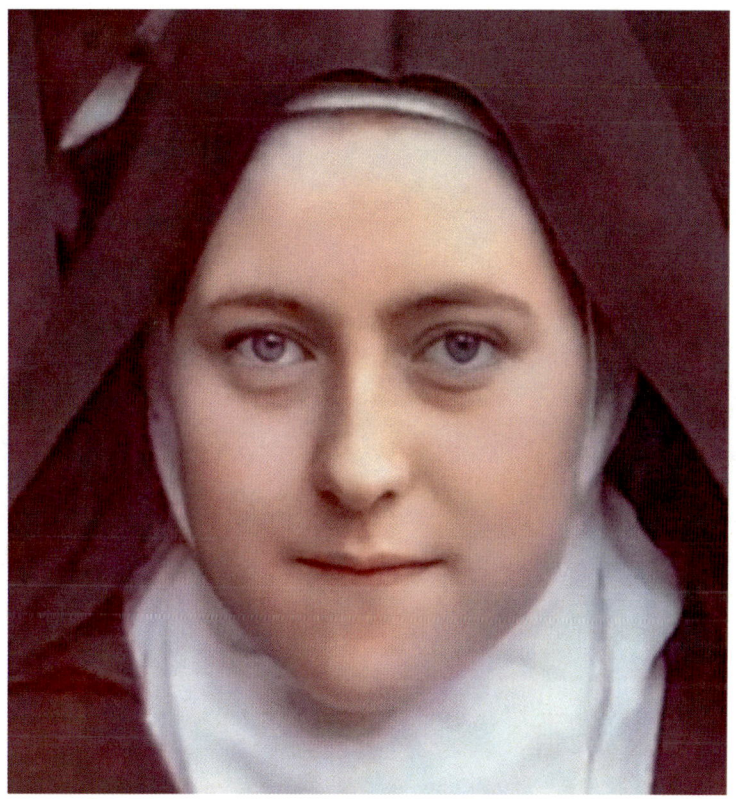

"I want to love God with all my being and make everyone else love Him." [20]

---

[20] Story of a Soul. ICS Publications. Washington D.C. Third edition. Chapter VIII

Without a doubt, we can define Saint Thérèse as the saint of immense desires. Her greatest desire was to be a saint, to love God with all her being, and to make Him be loved by all.

From this great desire, all her other desires emerged. She wanted to have all vocations, to be everything in the Church. In chapter nine of *"Story of a Soul"*, she describes her immense desires and writes: *"To be a spouse, oh Jesus, to be a Carmelite, to be through my union with You, the mother of souls, all this should be enough for me, but I feel within me other vocations: that of a warrior, that of a priest, that of an apostle, that of a doctor, that of a martyr... I would like to accomplish the most heroic deeds, I feel the courage of a crusader, and I would like to die on the battlefield in defense of the Church, the vocation of the priest... but alas, with all the desire to be a priest, I admire and envy the humility of St. Francis of Assisi and feel the vocation to imitate him by rejecting the sublime dignity of the priesthood... Oh, my beloved Jesus, how to reconcile these contrasts? How to make the desires of my poor soul a reality? If despite my smallness, I wanted to enlighten souls like the prophets and doctors... I have the vocation of an apostle... I would like to travel the earth, preach your name, and plant your glorious Cross in infidel soil, but my Beloved, one mission would not be enough for me. I would like to proclaim the Gospel at the same time in the five parts of the world, and even in the most remote islands... I would like to be a missionary not only for a few years but to have been so from the creation of the world and to continue to be so until the consummation of the ages... But above all and above everything, my beloved Savior, I would like to pour out for you to the last drop of my blood. Martyrdom! That is the dream of my youth... but I feel that this is another madness because I do not desire only one kind of martyrdom...; to satisfy me, I need them all... If I direct my thoughts to the unheard-of torments that the Christians suffered in the times of the Anti-Christ, I feel my heart shudder, and I would like all these torments to be reserved for me... Open, my Jesus, your book of life where the actions of all the saints are recorded, and I would like to perform all these exploits for You!"* [21]

St. Thérèse, faced with such immense desires, wonder how to achieve them being a cloistered nun, living in a convent without going out into the world at all. All of this seemed impossible, a true madness... but after much searching within herself, she discovered what she needed to satisfy all her immense desires within her vocation as a Discalced Carmelite.

My vocation is Love

"At last, I have found my vocation. My vocation is love. I realized that love encompasses all vocations, that love is everything, that love spans all times and all places, in a word, that love is eternal.[21]

Eureka! After turning it over and over in her mind, finally, Thérèse discovered the answer to her immense desires, and how to carry them out in her vocation. The answer was found precisely by reading the first Letter of Saint Paul to the Corinthians.

This epistle speaks about what love is, and it says:

"Though I speak with the tongues of men and of angels, and have not charity, I have become as sounding brass, or a tinkling

---

[21] Story of a Soul. ICS Publications. Washington D.C. Third edition pp. 192-193.

cymbal. And though I have the gift of prophecy, and understand all mysteries, and all knowledge; and though I have all faith, so that I could remove mountains, and have not charity, I am nothing. And though I bestow all my goods to feed the poor, and though I give my body to be burned, and have not charity, it profits me nothing. Charity suffers long and is kind; charity envies not; charity vaunts not itself, is not puffed up, do not behave itself unseemly, seeks not her own, is not easily provoked, thinks no evil; rejoices not in iniquity, but rejoices in the truth; bears all things, believes all things, hopes all things, endures all things. Charity never fails." (1 Cor. 13: 1-13)

When Thérèse read this epistle, she said it was as if a divine ray of light fell upon her, leading her to immense joy.

To carry out her vocation to love, Thérèse wrote a passage describing this process: "I have always wanted to be a saint, but when I compare myself with the great saints, **there is an abyss between them and me,** just as there is a difference between a mountain whose summit is lost in the clouds, and a tiny grain of sand trampled underfoot by passers-by. But **instead of getting discouraged** by this, I said to myself: **God cannot inspire**

unrealizable desires, so despite my littleness, I can aspire to holiness. It is impossible for me to grow on my own, **I must tolerate and accept myself as I am, with all my imperfections,** but I must find a way to reach heaven by a path that is straight, very short, a completely new way."[22]

I want an elevator to go to Heaven

In the time that Thérèse lived, elevators became fashionable among all the inventions, and on a trip to Rome with her father and her sister Celina, she was able to take the elevator of one of the hotels where they stayed. She was amazed to discover that, by using the elevator, she could climb stairs much more easily, and about this she wrote: "We are living now in an age of inventions, and we no longer have to take the trouble of climbing stairs, for, in the homes of the rich, an elevator has replaced these very successfully. I wanted to find an elevator which would raise me to Jesús, for I am too small to climb the rough stairway of perfection. I searched, then, in the Scriptures for some sign of this elevator, the object of my desires, and I read these words coming from the mouth of the Eternal Wisdom: *'Whoever is a little one, let him come to me.' (Prov. 9:4)*. And so, I succeeded. I felt I had found what I was looking for."[23]

"Oh, my God! what wouldn't you do for a little girl who approaches you; I kept searching and this is what I found: *'As a mother comfort her child, so I will comfort you; you shall be comforted in Jerusalem.'* (Is 66:12-13). Ah! never had such tender and melodious words come to rejoice my soul, the elevator that will take me to heaven is your arms, oh Jesus! **To reach perfection, I will not need to grow, on the contrary, I need to remain**

---

[22] Story of a Soul. ICS Publications. Washington D.C. Third edition pp. 207-208

small, to become smaller and smaller. Oh, my God! you have exceeded my expectations, and I want to sing your mercies[23]

Thérèse begins by saying that she had always wanted to be a saint. If you notice, the little way emphasizes the kindness and merciful love of God. It brought something new to her life by emphasizing this. Compared to the mentalities of her time it confronted her within the convent, as emphasis was placed on the justice of God, the severity of His demands, and the tendency to confuse holiness with extraordinary manifestations such as

---

[23] Ibid.

visions, ecstasies, and locutions, which, although they took place in some saints, are not the essence of holiness. This tendency encouraged the exclusion of ordinary and simple people from holiness because **holiness was considered a privilege only of some souls.**

St. Thérèse received the grace of restoring what holiness really is, taking away the idea that the people of her time had, restoring what God really proposes to us in the Gospel, and assuring us that holiness is for everyone, and it is accessible to everyone, just as St. Paul says in his letter to the Ephesians: *"For through him we both have access in one Spirit to the Father."* (Eph. 2:18)

Called to be saints

It is true that **to see God, we need to be saints.** I am sure that both you, me, and all Christians want to one day see Jesus and enjoy His eternal presence. Therefore, whether we know it or not, **there is a deep desire in us to become saints.**

St. Augustine, in his book of "Confessions," says:

> *"Lord, my heart is restless, it has a longing for you, and it will not rest until it rests in you."* [24]

This is true, our heart cannot be fully happy, completely satisfied until we are holy, until we can see God, and are united to Him forever.

Therefore, it is good to answer honestly the following questions:

---

[24] The Confessions of St. Augustine. transl., introduction. & notes, John K. Ryan. New York: Image Books. Book 1 Chapter 1

* What is the deepest desire of your heart?

* What are you currently aspiring to achieve?

* What do you think about becoming saint?

If your deepest desire is to love God, let Him love you, and make Him loved by others, then for sure you want to become a saint, and **you can be sure that you enjoy good spiritual health,** believing that God is always with you, and wants to help you achieve this desire, this great purpose.

Jesus wants to confirm to you that nothing and no one will never prevent you from achieving it, and that nothing, not even anyone in the world can separate you from God.

St. Paul affirms this in his Letter to the Romans by saying:

"For I am convinced that neither death nor life, nor angels nor demons, neither the present nor the future, nor any powers, neither height nor depth, nor anything else in all creation, will be able to separate us from the love of God that is in Christ Jesus our Lord."
(Rom 8:38-39)

The great paradox

Thérèse faced the great paradox **between her immense desires and her own physical and emotional fragility.** She had to tirelessly search for how to make her desires a reality.

At first, when she compared herself to the great saints, she thought that despite her good will and ardent desires what she wanted seemed impossible, as she quickly encountered her limitations, weaknesses, faults, and fragility.

The temptation was to feel that her desire to be holy was something inaccessible, something unattainable. In such a situation it was possible to get discouraged and think: "I will never be able to reach there." However, she reacted telling herself.

"God cannot inspire us with unrealizable desires, so despite my smallness, I can aspire to holiness." [25]

Today, we face something very difficult in our society which calls us to have great desires that **have nothing to do with God's desires.** We are taught in many ways to have things, live as we please, and achieve great power to be recognized, valued, and appreciated. **These are the three great temptations in which Jesus was in the desert.**

Nowadays, **we are also tempted in the same temptations** and see with great sadness how the desires to live according to God's plan are getting farther away from the proposals of the current world. What matters today is to **acquire material things, live according to our own pleasure, and seek ways to be powerful,** rich, and famous, without considering our spiritual life; as if we were only matter without spirit, when **we are embodied spirits.**

Self-acceptance

On her path to holiness, **the first thing Thérèse had to do was accept herself just as she was,** but, when trying to accept herself with her fragility, emotional instability, faults, and limitations, she realized that **she could not achieve her**

---

[25] Story of a Soul. ICS Publications. Washington D.C. Third edition p. 207

immense desires alone and needed God's help. suffered tremendously.

She writes: "if I happened to cause anyone, I loved some little trouble, even unwittingly, instead of forgetting about it and not crying, which made matters worse, I cried like a Magdalene and then when began to cheer up, I would begin to cry again for having cried."[26]

Indeed, **she was trapped in a very narrow circle from which she could not escape**. However, at the same time, she had a profound prayer life and a true desire for holiness.

Discovering this led her to want to live a **path of trust, love, and abandonment in God,** which represented a new phase in her life, a **change of perspective and vision;** in other words, a **conversion**, a true inner revolution that could give her the freedom she desired. Because of her hypersensitivity, she suffered tremendously.

---

[26] Story of a Soul. ICS Publications. Washington D.C. Third edition p. 207

It is a relief for us that she tells us about this stage of her life because possibly at some point, we too have been trapped in our own experiences of **suffering, with certain negative ideas and thoughts** that instead of helping us grow, encourage us to perceive ourselves and others as capable of moving forward despite our limitations.

Life's trials can make us succumb and discourage us, making us believe that we are incapable and powerless to emerge victorious from our inner battles.

Let us remember what **Eric Berne** told us about **the perception we have of reality, ourselves, others, and even God, as that will color our lives, filling them with light or darkness.**

As mentioned earlier, when Thérèse was fourteen years old, she needed to be healed emotionally. The smile of the Virgin Mary healed her physically, but she had to wait some more years to receive the grace she called **"the grace of Christmas" which pulled her out of her painful situation of emotional instability.**

She narrates how this happened during Christmas Eve Mass when, after receiving Communion, **the Lord inspired her to act bravely and overcome her hypersensitivity.** She writes how on that night God worked a little miracle to make her grow up in an instant. "On that luminous night, Jesus, the gentle, little Child of only one hour, changed the night of my soul into rays of light... **since that night, I have never been defeated in any combat,** but rather walked from victory to victory, beginning so to speak, "To run as a giant."[27]

---

[27] Ibid. p.97

This great gift she received that Christmas, **gave her the strength to receive her inner healing**, and regained the emotional health she had lost since her mother's death.

After receiving that healing and inner liberation, Thérèse says **"I began the third period of my life, the most beautiful and the most filled with graces from heaven. The work I had been unable to do in ten years was done by Jesus in one instant."** She was then able to embark, as she celebrates herself, on a wonderful and brave desire to enter the Carmelite Convent of the city of Lisieux.

She was then able to embark, as she celebrates herself, on a wonderful and brave desire to enter the Carmelite Convent of the city of Lisieux.

I share all of this with you not only so that you can learn more about the personality, life, struggles of Saint Thérèse, but also so that you realize how **God can perform great healings when we least expect it.**

Sometimes God calls us to step out of ourselves, to take a few steps forward, and to become more mature, free, and happy people. Like now, in this retreat, where **we approach Jesus, our doctor of body and soul, and ask him with all our heart to heal us.**

The process of conversion and sanctification

Perhaps like Thérèse, sometimes we have been going round and round in our minds about difficult situations that keep us locked in our immaturity, complaints, anxieties, fears, shortcomings, dependencies, and sins, until suddenly one day we receive the grace of the Holy Spirit´s action, which surprises us and comes to set us free. It is then that we must choose whether we want to change, as Saint Thérèse did.

It is for the Holy Spirit to heal us, that we must be determined to carry out our conversion, the change we need for our life to be free, and holly.

This reminds me of something from my own story that I now share with you.

For years, I was a heavy smoker. I started smoking first because it was trendy, but then I took up smoking as my "lifeline" when I was in the very painful situation of seeing my marriage falling apart. I became tied to cigarettes for years and couldn't let go.

In that condition, I began to approach Jesus, with my cigarette... I started to desire to compose songs for him and became a "mariachi" of the Lord, as I called myself, because I was the one who animated my prayer group with songs from my guitar. However, the cigarette bothered me, because I couldn't smoke while I played, and I also started to cough because of the nicotine entering my lungs. Without realizing it, Jesus was there with me, receiving my songs, my smoke and living closer to me than I imagined...

At that time, I was invited to participate in a Healing Congress organized by Christian psychologists in Houston, Texas. I decided to go with a friend, hoping to listen to Father Francis MacNutt, a Dominican priest who was very well known for his healing gift.

In the years leading up to that Congress, the desire to quit smoking had been growing in me, in large part because my children started telling me that, in their school, they had been told how harmful smoking was, not only for those of us who smoked, but for everyone around us. Of course, that comment was directed at me, making me see that every time I smoked, I was harming them, contaminating not only the environment but also harming everyone around me, including them and of course myself.

I had not been able to quit smoking on my own, but God used that Congress to heal me through the prayer that Father Francis. I remember with great gratitude that at the beginning of the Congress, a Eucharist was celebrated, and during it, Father Francis asked us if we had any "desire" that we wanted God to grant us. Of course, inwardly I said "yes", and at that moment I asked Jesus to free me from my dependence on cigarettes. I told Him that I wanted to follow Him without being attached to that horrible habit.

I approached the altar where many of us went to ask Father Francis to pray for us, and when it was my turn, he looked deeply into my eyes, and laid his hands on me while praying in tongues. Suddenly, I felt a force coming from above towards me, and it was so strong that it threw me to the ground. I then fell into a kind of sleep in which I saw myself in the grotto of Bethlehem, where Jesus was born, and next to him, I was lying in His manger.

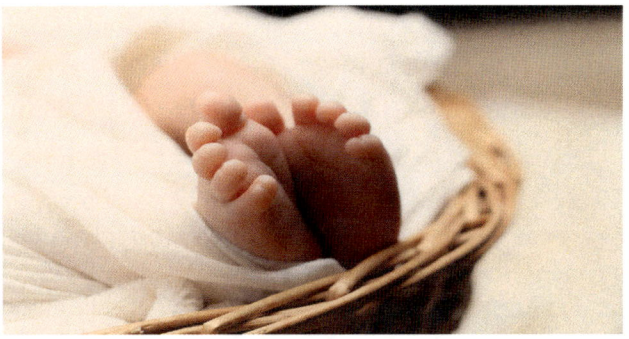

While I slept, I heard Virgin Mary singing a most beautiful lullaby, and then she took me in her arms, rocked me, and placed me in St. Joseph's arms, while she took Baby Jesus in her arms and continued singing the beautiful melody that rocked us and filled us with peace.

I don't know how long I spent in that rest of the Spirit, but when I woke up, the experience of being a smoker had completely disappeared from my mind. It was something fabulous.

It was something fabulous. At the end of the Mass, I returned to my room, threw away the pack of cigarettes I had, and since then, I have not felt the need to smoke again.

God, through the Holy Family, had taken care of healing me through Father Francis' prayer. I truly believe that when we ask God to heal us, He knows how and when to do it. Blessed be Our Lord!

I share this with you because I believe it is important to remember that **God always listens to our desires, and if they are for our good, they will be fulfilled.**

He always wants the best for us. The only thing He asks of us is to share our situation with Him, so that He can work His great work of healing in our smallness. He wants to change our hearts, minds, attitudes, and lives. His desire is to heal and convert us, so we can make an act of courage even in small things. He wants to free us from everything that separates us from Him and prevents us from growing humanly and spiritually.

Saint Thérèse first had to accept herself as she was, and then **accept to change by placing herself in God's hands** so that He could help her make that life change. This act of bravery is what we also need to do.

Here are some questions for you:

* Do you accept yourself for who you are?

* Do you accept your flaws and limitations?

* Do you accept that you are a sinner?

* Do you really believe that God loves you unconditionally?

* Do you trust that He wants to transform you if you ask Him to do so?

Today, I invite you to **free yourself from all your guilt and fears** that may be preventing you from being embraced by God's immense, faithful, and unconditional love. Remember that **God always has compassion for our misery,** for mercy means exactly that. He has compassion for our misery so much that He came into the world, suffered, and died so that we may have **abundant and eternal life in Him.**

In the process of healing, conversion, and sanctification, you are not alone. We all need some inner healing, and we all need to turn to God to fight the battle that we must fight in the world with Him; so, **let us do our part and let God do His part** giving us the victory that sanctifies us.

Being a Christian is not easy, especially in these times when the world would like us to forget about God completely and seduces us to do our will instead of His; yet, everything we experience, good or bad, easy, or difficult, our defeats and our successes, **Saint Thérèse says, all is grace** and all we live is part of our process of conversion, transformation, and sanctification. Saint Paul reminds us that saying:

"We know that in all things God works for good for those who love Him." (Rom 8:28-32)

"Yes": the most important word in the Gospels

When we believe in God and love Him, we want to say **"Yes"** to what He asks of us because we want to please Him, knowing that His will is always the best for us, even if sometimes we may not understand it, or it is difficult to fulfill.

I always say that **the most important word in the Gospel,** and the shortest one of only one syllable, is **"Yes" to God´s will.** It is the **"Yes"** of Virgin Mary in the Annunciation.

When we say **"Yes"** to God, He gives us the courage to gradually change through the Holy Spirit´s action and continue our process to become saints through Him.

Holiness is primarily the work of God in us, our part is to let Him make us holy. This is precisely the secret of the way of spiritual childhood that Saint Thérèse teaches us: **surrender to God with complete trust and love, as his little children**, so that in His arms we discover that **He loves us like no one else can love us and let Him change in us what keeps us away from Him.**

"Behold the handmaid of the Lord; be it done to me according to thy word." (Lk 1:38)

Let's never forget that Virgin Mary's "Yes" to the will of God was the blessed door that opened the way to our salvation!

To reflect on the continued Yes of Mary, Jesus, and Joseph, I give you this video.

"Mary, the Mother of Jesus"

https://tinyurl.com/24xvsnee

The need to be humble

When I talk to you about the importance of saying **Yes to God**, I think of **the first step that alcoholics must take** when they start their rehabilitation at Alcoholics Anonymous program. [28]

The first thing they must do is to be humble and acknowledge that they cannot stop drinking by themselves, that they need a "higher power" to help them let go of alcohol. They **must accept their personal incapacity to change on their own** and the need to **rely on that higher power to overcome their drinking.**

Alcoholics must face their illness with a **humble recognition** of the reality of their powerlessness. This awareness is the **secure foundation** upon which they can receive the grace to begin rebuilding their lives, following the liberating process of the remaining eleven steps. That first step, **that "Yes", is essential because without it, the others could not be taken.**

---

[28] en.Wikipedia.org Alcoholics_ Anonymous

Accepting our weaknesses and faults also helps us to **accept those of others.** By confronting our difficulty in changing, we can more easily understand the difficulty of others. Sometimes we suffer a lot and tire ourselves out trying to change others, but we forget that the first thing we need to do is learn to be humble, **accept our weaknesses and ask God to help us change.** That awareness, will help us learn to accept others with their weaknesses and **to pray for ourselves and for them**, trusting that little by little, with God's help, we will change and so will others. This is the secret to living together in peace and harmony, whether with our family, friends, colleagues, or anyone else.

Note that becoming a convert and following the path of spiritual childhood requires not only our desire for healing and conversion, but also humility, much patience, time, effort, prayer, and a **"determined determination** [29]to keep growing, as Saint

---

[29] Interior Castle. Dover Publications. New York. Chapter 1

Teresa of Jesus, the great saint and spiritual master of Avila, would say.

It's like wanting to prepare a banquet with delicious dishes. First, we need to learn the art of good cooking following the training of a good chef. This will be the best way, to do it with knowledge, without wasting time, effort, and with great love and desire to please our guests. And something very important; the dishes that we prepare praying while cooking will not only delight the palates of our guests but will also contain the most powerful ingredient to feed their souls: our prayer for their needs, bringing God´s love and healing to those who eat them.

Likewise, in the spiritual life, it is important that we learn how to take the fastest, most direct, and shortest path that Saint Thérèse, our "spiritual chef," proposes, so that we can enjoy the banquet that God has prepared for and share it with others.

Rs.

Questions for your reflection

In this spiritual spa that you are carrying out, ask Jesus:

* Lord, what is the **"Yes"** that you ask of me today?

* What small act of courage and trust do I need to do to grow humanly and spiritually?

* What door do I need to open in my heart, in my mind, and in my whole being so that the Holy Spirit may enter and change me from within?

You can be sure that if you give your "Yes" to God, His sanctifying grace will certainly visit you, touch you, and heal whatever needs to be healed in you, in your relationships with others, and of course, in your relationship with Him.

It is a fact that God wants to give you that strength and liberation, but to receive them, you need to learn to say "Yes" to Him, in something perhaps small, or big, but your "Yes" is very important for the Holy Spirit to act and give you the gifts you need. Be sure that He will take care of healing and sanctifying you in due time.

The light of the Word of God

Remember that I shared with you earlier, that Thérèse went on a trip to Rome with her father and her sister Celine, and thinking about her smallness, said to herself "How I would like to find an elevator that would take me up to Jesus, since I am too small to climb the steep ladder of perfection."

Where do you think she found that elevator?

Wisely, she went to look for it in the Bible.

In her book "Story of a Soul", she narrates how through the Word of God she found the answer she was anxiously seeking.

Thérèse had a great love for Sacred Scripture; all the lights that were guiding her on her path, and all her great intuitions, she found them there. Every time a question troubled her, she went to find the answer in the Word of God. **She anticipated what the Second Vatican Council saw as the importance of promoting the study of the Bible among all believers.**

This is another of her great teachings. When we value something, **when something truly interests us, we want to learn more about it.** If we do this at the human level, we are mostly called to do it at the spiritual level. What better way then, than to become familiar with the **Word of God,** which is not something but **Someone. It is Our Lord, who speaks to us.** We need to listen carefully to what He says and what He wants to convey to us, so that we know which direction to take on the path of our life and not get lost. How many times, when we are confused, the answer comes to us through the Word of God.

Every time we participate in the Eucharist, God has a **personal message** in His Word for each one of us; a call that seeks to form our conscience, respond to critical situations we may be going through, encourage us, and teach us to live His way. **Do we really listen attentively to His Word, as if He were personally addressing it to each one of us?**

The Word of God is like a compass, always there to guide us towards the good, but to discover His message, we need our ears to be attentive. I do not only mean through our sense of hearing, but also to be attentive and interested, **listening with our mind and our heart."**

For the word of God is living and active, sharper than any two-edged sword, piercing to the division of soul and of spirit, of joints and of marrow, and discerning the thoughts and intentions of the heart." (Hebrews 4:12)

Communication with God, as all **communication, is an art that we must learn.** We need to learn how to **enter in a dialogue with Him, back and forth**. When we read or listen to the Word of God, **it is not just about receiving information.**

What is important is that we reflect on it with our mind and listen to it with the ears of our heart. **It is not just about receiving what it says, but letting that it penetrates in us**, that we understand it according to all our circumstances, because its message is directed to everyone, but at the same time it is directed to each one of us.

Jesus´s little bird

In Story of a Soul, at the end of Manuscript B, St. **Thérèse compares herself to a little bird,** and in this comparison offers us **central teachings in her spirituality** that can serve as a wise guide for your life. I recommend that you **take the time to calmly reflect on each of her teachings,** so that you can engrave them in your heart and mind and get the most out of them.

She says about herself: "I consider myself a weak little bird covered only by a light down. I am not an eagle, I only have the eyes and heart of an eagle, for despite my extreme smallness I dare to gaze steadily at the divine Sun, the Sun of love, and my heart feels within it all the aspirations of the eagle.[30]

It is interesting that she says that being a weak little bird, she is not like an eagle, but nevertheless, she has the eyes and heart of an eagle. **Yes, eyes to contemplate Jesus, and heart to love Him.**

Ask yourself:

* Who do your eyes look at?

* Who does your heart love?

* Have you ever felt looked upon and loved by Jesus?

She continues the comparison saying: "The little bird would like to fly towards that brilliant Sun that dazzles its eyes; it would like to imitate its sisters, the Eagles, which it sees rising towards the divine focus of the Holy Trinity... but, alas, the most it can do is raise its wings, but flying is not within its modest power!

What will become of it? Will it die of grief at seeing itself so powerless? Oh no! the little bird will not even become

---

[30] Story of a Soul. ICS Publications, Washington D.C. Third Edition pp.198-200

disheartened; with bold abandonment, it wants to continue gazing fixedly at its divine Sun. Nothing will be able to frighten it, neither the wind nor the rain. And if the dark clouds were to hide from it the Star of love, the little bird will not change its place: it knows that beyond the clouds its Sun continues to shine, and that its radiance cannot be eclipsed for an instant.

It is true that, at times, the little bird's heart is assailed by the storm, and it seems to it that nothing else can exist but the clouds that surround it. That is the hour of perfect joy for this poor and weak creature... what happiness for it to continue there despite everything, gazing fixedly at the invisible light that is hidden from its faith ...!" [31]

Let's look at the key points that St. Thérèse talks about in this comparison.

1. The importance of knowing ourselves.

Carl Rogers[32], the well known American humanistic psychologist, writes in his book *"On Becoming a Person"* about three elements that help us know ourselves: **Self-concept, self-esteem, and the "ideal self"**.

Self-concept is the image we have of ourselves, what we see in ourselves, both positive and negative. **This image is influenced by our relationship mainly with our parents, relatives, and very important people in our lives.**

The self-concept we have of ourselves may or may not be real and may be distorted, making us see ourselves as something we are not, whether the image we have is superior to reality or

---

[31] Ibid. p. 198

[32] https://en.wikipedia.org/wiki/Carl_Rogers

inferior to it. Our self-concept is dynamic, and therefore **we can change it** depending on the reinterpretation we give to our personality, experiences, and external judgments we receive.

Self-esteem has to do with **the way we value ourselves** and is based on the self-concept we **have. In terms of this, factors such as comparing** ourselves to others, the opinion that others have of us according to how they respond positively or negatively to who we are and what we do will influence whether we develop positive or negative self-esteem.

The **"ideal self"** is the idealized image we have of ourselves that **serves as motivation and guidance for our behavior.** This image is based on past experiences and on expectations and influences both, family, cultural, social, and religious.

Let's reflect on how St. Thérèse lived these three concepts:

She begins her comparison by saying: "I consider myself a weak little bird covered only by a light down. **I am not an eagle, I only have eagle eyes and heart**, for despite my extreme smallness, I dare to stare fixedly at the divine Sun, the Sun of Love, and my heart feels within itself all the aspirations of an eagle."

In Thérèse, we see that her self-concept aligns with reality. She recognizes herself as small, fragile, and weak, as she has been since birth, having to face her fragile health both physically and emotionally. However, this does not make her feel inferior. **She acknowledges that although she is not an eagle, she has the eyes and heart of an eagle.**

Thérèse by getting to know herself, achieved a healthy self-esteem, as we see that although she knows she is small, she values herself and knows she is unconditionally loved and valued by God, and likewise, she has been shown much love in her family. All of this makes her realize that she is valuable and strengthens her to move forward as that "fragile and weak little bird, but at the same time strong and brave."

The "ideal self" in Saint Thérèse is present within herself and she manifests it by **wanting to find ways to be better every day. Her ideal is to please and love God, and to love and serve others**; thus, she confesses that although she is not an eagle, she has all the aspirations of an eagle.

Saint Thérèse, through her life testimony, **teaches us the importance of knowing ourselves as we are,** without trying to be someone else. **Self-awareness is essential to become aware of what we are and what we are not.** Sometimes we want to be like other people, we compare ourselves to them, and we feel inferior. Other times we may feel superior to someone else, and both are mistakes that prevent us from seeing clearly what we really are and realizing that each of us is unique and unrepeatable.

God loves us just as we are, with our faults and qualities. Therefore, **it is good to see ourselves through His eyes** so that **He can free us from our complexes, whether of superiority or inferiority,** and help us become the people we are called to be **according to His unique plan for each of us."**

Ask yourself:

* How do you see yourself?

* Do you value yourself?

* Do you compare yourself to others?

* What do you reject about yourself?

* What do you like about yourself?

* Who do your eyes look at?

* Who does your heart love?
* Have you felt looked at or loved by Jesus?
* What aspirations do you have?
* What does Saint Thérèse teach you about this?

2. Our longings and realities.

Saint Thérèse says, "The little bird wants to fly towards the Sun that dazzles its eyes; it wants to imitate its sisters, the eagles, which it sees soaring towards the divine focus of the Most Holy Trinity... But alas! The most it can do is lift its wings, but that of flying is not within its modest power!"[33]

This second teaching emphasizes how, like Saint Thérèse, we probably have those great desires inside us to imitate people who are role models for us, like in our case, the desire to imitate Thérèse.

The desire to imitate her is excellent, but let us remember that we are not her, and therefore it is good to want to imitate her

---

[33] Ibid p. 198

virtues, but to be ourselves without trying to be her, because we are not. **So, value who you are.**

Saint Thérèse imitated her founder, Saint Teresa of Ávila, in many ways, but realizing that she had to do it from her own personality. So do each one of us. Of course, we are called to follow the teachings of Saint Thérèse, but from who you, I, and each one of us is, and according to the unique path that God traces for each one. **Saint Thérèse recognized her limitations and what she could or could not do.**

* Do you recognize your talents?
* Do you take advantage of them?
* Do you recognize your limitations?
* What does Saint Thérèse teach you about this?

3. Let us not be disheartened by our limitations.

Saint Thérèse had to face her limitations and, finding herself unable to be like the great saints, whom she compares to eagles, and feeling like a small and weak little bird, she says: "What will become of him? Will he die of sorrow to see himself so impotent...? Nothing will frighten him, neither wind nor rain. And even if dark clouds come to hide from him the star of love, the little bird will not change place: he knows that beyond the clouds his Sun still shines and that its radiance cannot be eclipsed for an instant."[34]

When we go through situations in our lives where we feel overwhelmed and incapable, **the easiest thing is to give up**, but precisely what Saint. Thérèse teaches us is not to be disheartened,

---

[34] Ibid. p. 98

but to trust in God, not allowing ourselves to become depressed and downtrodden.

* Do you get discouraged when you realize your limitations?

* What do you do if you do not get the results that are expected of you?

4. What to do during life's storms.

Saint Thérèse tells us: "It is true that sometimes the heart of the little bird is buffeted by the storm, and it does not seem that there can be anything other than the clouds that surround it. That is the hour of perfect joy for that poor and weak being. What happiness for him to continue there, despite everything, gazing fixedly at the invisible light that is hidden from his faith!"

Let us remember the account given by Saint Matthew when he narrates in the Gospel, how on one occasion Jesus got into a boat with his disciples, and suddenly a great storm arose on the sea, so that the boat was covered by the waves; but he was asleep. And they came to him and woke him, saying:

"Lord, save us, we are perishing!" He said to them, *"Why are you afraid, O you of little faith?" Then he got up, rebuked the winds and the sea, and there was a great calm.* (Mt 8:23-26)

This teaching contains great wisdom, for it will be precisely in times of great trials and sufferings when Saint Thérèse advises us not to stop looking at Jesus, not to stop believing in Him, to hope in Him, remembering that beyond the "clouds" and in the midst of our storms, our fears and anxieties, He is with us, accompanies us on the journey of life, cares for us, and continues to love us faithfully, **especially when we go through great trials and sufferings.**

* What are you afraid of?

* What things can cause anxiety or distress in you?

* Where or in whom do you take refuge when things don't go well

* Do you trust that God watches over you, during your storms?

* What do you learn from Saint Thérèse about this?

5. Our failures.

In the comparison that Thérèse makes about the little bird, she also says: "Many times the imperfect little creature, although staying in its place (under the rays of the Sun), **ends up getting a little distracted from its only task**: picking a grain here and there, chasing after a worm...; then finding a puddle of water, it wets its newly formed feathers in it; it sees a flower that it likes, and its weak spirit is entertained by the flower... In short, the poor little bird, unable to soar like the eagles, continues to be entertained by the trivialities of the earth.

However, after all its misbehavior, instead of hiding in a corner to cry its misery and die of regret, the little bird turns to its beloved Sun, exposes its wet wings to its beneficent rays, moans like the swallow; and in its sweet song, it confides and recounts in detail its infidelities, thinking of its reckless abandonment, to acquire greater dominion and attract with greater fullness the love of Him who did not come to seek the righteous but sinners..." [35]

The greatest pain we can feel knowing that we are totally loved by God is to fail Him.

Saint Thérèse teaches us that, although we may fall repeatedly and sin, we cannot give up, for **God knows the mud we are made of and is always ready to forgive us when we return repentant and ask for forgiveness.**

This reminds me of **the parable of the Prodigal Son** when the younger son, after asking his father to give him the part of his fortune, left home, and squandered his money on a life of debauchery. Later, when he had spent it all, he experienced a severe famine, and coming to his senses realized how he had failed his father. **Repenting of his bad deeds, he then decided to return home to ask for his father's forgiveness.**

We read in the gospel: "While he was still a long way off, his father saw him and was moved with pity. He ran to the boy,

---

[35] Ibid. p.199

clasped him in his arms and kissed him. Then his son said, 'Father, I have sinned against **heaven** and against you. I no longer deserve to be called your son'. But the father said to his servants, "Quick! Bring out the best robe and put it on him; put a ring on his finger and sandals on his feet. Bring the calf we have been fattening and kill it; we will celebrate by having a feast, **because this son of mine was dead and has come back to life; he was lost and is found,** and they began to celebrate." (Lk 15: 11-32)

Questions for you:

* Do you find it difficult to acknowledge your mistakes?

* What do you do when you make a mistake?

* Do you repent and ask for forgiveness from those you have offended?

* Can you forgive those who have harmed you in some way, or do you hold grudges and resentment towards them?

6. Remaining confident in God's love during our trials and sufferings.

Saint Thérèse tells us: "And if the beloved remains deaf to the pitiful chirping of its little creature, remains hidden ..., well then, the little creature will continue to be there, soaked, will accept being frozen with cold, and will continue to rejoice in that suffering which it has really deserved." [36]

As we saw earlier, **the conversion, purification, and liberation of our being is a process that takes time, much patience, prayer, and a change of vision.** It is a great comfort to strengthen our faith, hope, and love for God, for **He watches over us throughout the process** and knows that the Holy Spirit will be helping us to change and purify us in the love we need to be transformed.

* Do you trust in God even if He doesn't immediately fulfill your requests during your trials and sufferings?

* Do you despair when you fall into the same faults again and again?

* Do you believe that prayer can help heal your wounds?

7. The blessing of being and remaining small.

Saint Thérèse tells us: "How happy, Jesus, is Your little bird of being weak and small! For what would it be if it were great...? It

---

[36] Ibid. p.199

would never have the audacity to appear in Your presence, to doze off before You..." [37]

She encourages us to be small, to not be afraid, and to always trust in Jesus' loving and provident care. She teaches us how **love begets humility in our lives and emphasizes the need for us to recognize our own weakness and dependence on God,** to learn to see ourselves with humility from God's perspective, as wisely said by **Saint Teresa of Avila,** to see ourselves truthfully because **"humility is walking in truth."**

This requires a true knowledge of ourselves that helps us accept our smallness and **value the gifts that God has given us, which come not from ourselves but from Him.** Therefore, seeing ourselves as small before God leads us to **recognize our need for His grace and to realize that He is our strength in our weakness.**

* Why do you think Saint Thérèse speaks of humility when recommending that we be small?

* What does Jesus' statement "His strength is made perfect in our weakness" mean to you?

* Write your own definition of humility.

* What do you learn from Saint Thérèse about this?

Here she encourages us to have faith in God's love during times of trial and suffering. Saint Thérèse's quote emphasizes that even if God seems distant and our prayers unanswered, we should.

8. During trial, nothing better than surrendering ourselves to God.

---

[37] Ibid.

Saint Thérèse says: if she were great, she would never have the audacity to doze off in front of God. "Yes, this is also another weakness of the little bird when he wants to stare fixedly at the divine Sun and the clouds do not let him see a single ray: despite himself, his little eyes close, his head hides under his wing, and the poor thing falls asleep believing to continue staring fixedly at his beloved Star."[38]

Saint Thérèse speaks to us about moments in our lives **when we cannot find a way out of our problems,** and in those circumstances, **the best thing to do is not to worry but to trust and surrender ourselves to God's divine providence,** which will come to meet us at the right moment.

When we make decisions in that state of darkness, it is possible that we make mistakes, so **she advises us to wait for the Lord to clarify our situation and open new possibilities for us.** Therefore, it is best to **follow these four things:**

Trust, surrender to His love, wait, and pray.

* When have you been in a situation that overwhelmed you?
* What did you do to resolve it?
* How much patience do you have during trials?
* Do you know how to rest in Jesus' arms?
* What does Saint Therese recommend doing in this case?

9. The importance of our prayer.

And regarding this, Saint Thérèse says that when the little bird wakes up after dozing off in front of Our Lord, "he does not despair, his little heart remains at peace, and he begins his duty

---

[38] Ibid. p. 199

of love again. He invokes the angels and the saints, who rise like eagles towards the devouring Focus, the object of their desires, and the eagles, feeling sorry for their little brother, protect and defend him, and put to flight the vultures that would like to devour him.

Prayer is always the bridge that leads us to encounter Jesus.

Saint Thérèse teaches us to always remain in prayer, giving Jesus every moment of our life, but, **when we go through stages of confusion, trials, and sufferings**, it is especially important that we **intensify our prayer**, also asking for the help and intercession of the Blessed Virgin, the angels, and the saints, for they will surely intercede for us, especially the Virgin Mary

and Saint Thérèse, since Our Lady is our mother and best intercessor before God, and Saint Thérèse is our spiritual guide in this retreat.

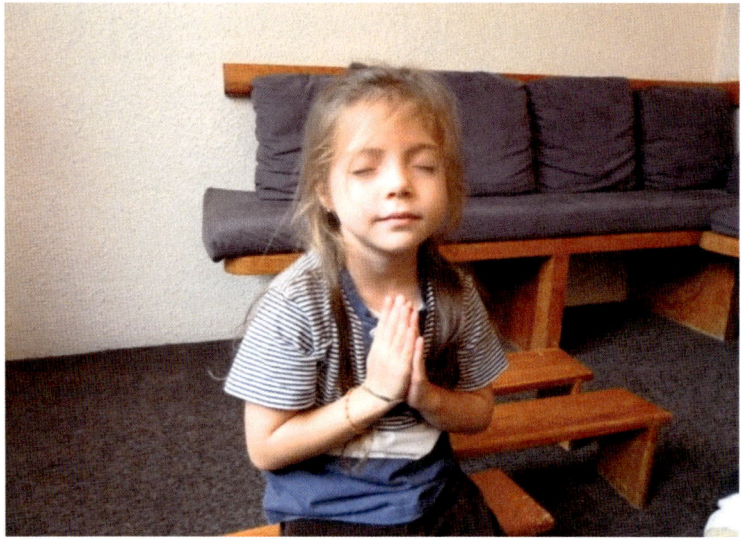

* Do you have a special time for prayer?

* Do you pray every day?

* What is your prayer like?

* Which saints do you entrust yourself to in your prayer?

* What do you learn from Saint Thérèse regarding this?

10. Let's not be afraid of vultures, enemies of Love.

This is what Saint Thérèse says: **"The little bird does not fear the vultures, images of demons, for it is not destined to be their prey**, but that of the Eagle who contemplates it in the center of the Sun of love... Eternal Eagle, you want to nourish me with your divine substance, me, a poor and insignificant being who would return to nothingness if your divine gaze did not give me life at every moment! Jesus, let me tell you, in the excess of my gratitude, let me, yes, tell you that your love reaches madness... How can my heart not be drawn to you in the face of that madness? How can my trust know any limits...?" [39]

With her words of intense love, **Saint Thérèse makes a definitive call for trust in God's love, which loves us madly, from always and forever.** It is this love that leads her to trust, to be bold, to surrender herself to God without measure.

Let us ask her to intercede for us so that we too may have that audacity to love Jesus with all our being, **always trusting in him and without fear of the attacks of evil.**

* How have you faced evil in your life?

* Are you afraid of the snares of evil?

* What do Saint Thérèse's beautiful words to Jesus tell you?

* What does Saint Thérèse invite you to do?

---

[39] Ibid. p.199

11. Remaining in God´s love eternally.

Thérèse continues to tell Jesus: "My madness consists in begging my eagle sisters to obtain for me the grace to fly towards the Sun of love with the divine Eagle's own wings... For as long as you want, my Beloved, your little bird will remain without strength and without wings, **will continue to keep its eyes fixed on you. It wants to be fascinated by your divine gaze, wants to be prey to your love...** One day, as I hope, the beloved Eagle will come to seek your little bird; and soaring with him to the Focus of love, you **will immerse him for all eternity in the burning abyss of that love** to which he offered himself as a victim." [40]

Saint Thérèse here reminds us how her work is precisely to love Jesus madly, and in her smallness, to plead with the saints to be able to fly with the wings of Jesus, her divine Eagle.

In this last passage of her meditation, she goes back to the final desire of her earthly life, **with the certainty that one day, the divine Eagle will come to fetch her and carry her on its wings to the fullness of life and love.**

We have been created by the love of God and we are precious in his eyes. Let´s never forget that we are not called to death but to life, abundant and eternal life.

For God so loved the world that he gave his one and only Son, that whoever believes in him shall not perish but have eternal life. (1 Jn 5:11)

---

[40] Ibid. p. 200

Saint Thérèse immerses us in her dialogue of love with Jesus, **encouraging us to remember that God always takes the initiative to love us** and lead us so that we finally desire what He desires, and love him with all our being. It will be precisely the mutual love between Him and each of us what will finally crown our life and the lives of others into **eternal happiness.**

At the end of her short life, while gazing at her crucifix she pronounced very distinctively: *"Oh! I love Him!"* and a moment later! My *God, I love You!* Suddenly her eyes came to life and were fixed on a spot just a little above the statue of the Blessed Virgin. Her face took the appearance it had when Thérèse enjoyed good health. She seemed to be in ecstasy... Then she closed her eyes and expired" [41]

Remaining in Jesus´s love forever

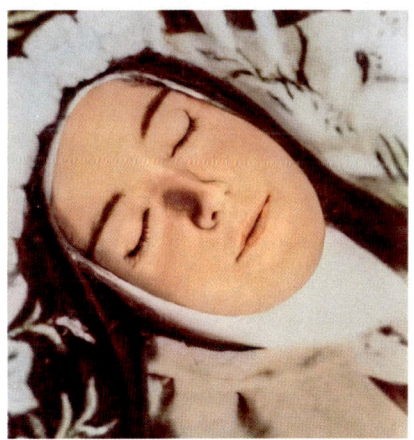

"I am not dying, I´m entering into Life" [42]

---

[41] Ibid. p. 271

[42] Ibid.

Questions for your reflection

* What would it mean for you to reach the goal at the end of your life?

* What grace does Saint Thérèse wanted to obtain from the saints?

* How do you imagine your life after death?

* How can you prepare for it?

Time for prayer

Ask the Holy Spirit to give you new insights, more flavor to your life, more freedom, more peace, and more joy. Give yourself time for your encounter with Jesus in the silence of your heart to become more vivid and closer now that he calls you and says: **"Come to Me!"**

Look closely at the images I am going to present to you. Imagine and feel as if it were you who is there, opening your arms **to receive the embrace of Jesus, and welcoming his embrace with all your soul and heart.**

Remember that imagination is faster than the speed of light. When you see the image, stay there, contemplate it... carefully... attentively. Pay attention to every detail, to the expression of her and him. What are they telling you? What emotion is in them? Imagine what they are thinking and saying.

Contemplate the landscape, the colors, and the shapes. What do you think of them? What do they remind you of? Where do they take you? In your imagination, embrace Jesus, and let yourself be embraced by him, rest in him, receive his embrace and hold him tight in your arms.

Give Jesus any problems you have, your tiredness, your sorrows and sufferings, your fragility, your sins, and **let His love comfort you, strengthen you, heal you and sanctify you.**

Give Him your joy, your gratitude, for his presence in your life and in this retreat, you have made, talk to him about what you want to give Him, everything you do and what you hope to accomplish.

Ask Him for what you need and let him inspire and guide you to carry out His will in your life.

Now, I invite you to watch and enjoy this video on such an important topic as being aware of what pleases God.

Video: My Song of Today

https://tinyurl.com/496rpwhd

¡Come to Me!

My Jesus, upon receiving your embrace,

I will embrace and love others in your Name

New desires

Dear reader, after this unforgettable encounter with Jesus, it is time to end our spiritual spa. I want to congratulate you for having completed it. My greatest wish is that St. Thérèse, by her testimony of life and her little way of spiritual childhood has encouraged you to follow her spirituality, so that you continue growing in love of God and others. I´m sure that through these pages Jesus has made himself present in you, allowing you to savor the delights of His love, and painting His image in your soul, so that with Him you can conquer your great dreams.

I´m preparing a second Spiritual Spa to be published. In it, we will continue delving into new and rich topics of St. Thérèse´s spirituality, like the one she calls: **"the science of love".** This second spiritual spa will be full of great surprises and blessings for your soul, so I hope to find you there and continue growing together on the path towards fullness. For now, if you have enjoyed and benefited from this experience, I invite you to share it with your family, friends, and contacts, remembering that **when we receive a great gift from God, He wants us to give it to others, and lead them to the encounter of His everlasting love.**

Receive with these new desires my prayer wrapped in a loving embrace.

Angelina Muñiz-Liedo

Jesus, allow my lips never to seal, so I keep proclaiming your immense Love

Prayer in honour of St. Thérèse

O Saint Thérèse of the Child Jesus,
seeing what confidence I have in God,
kindly present my intentions before the merciful Lord,
whom you behold face to face.

Intercede for me with the Blessed Virgin Mary,
who came to smile on you when you were suffering.

Looking on those who pray to you,
and on all those undergoing distress and trials,
I unite myself to them as my brothers and sisters.

Show yourself to be our sister and pour on us a shower of roses.

Ask the Lord to grant the graces we desire, if it be his will,
and make us stronger in faith, hope, and love on the road to
life.

Help us to follow your "Little Way of Spiritual Childhood",
trusting in the mercy and love of God like a little child,
as you learned from Jesus himself.

Give us a thirst for Holy Scripture,
a hunger for the Sacraments of the Church,
and passionate self-giving love for our neighbours,
that like you we may be love in the heart of the Church.

May we be assisted at the moment of death,
so that we pass from this world into the peace of God our
Father and know the eternal joy of the children of God.

Amen.

Welcome!

 @AngelinaMuñiz-Liedo

 @AngelinaMLiedoEscritora

 @angelinamunizliedo

 @angelina74624665

 @angelinamuniz-liedo3532

 angelina@vidahumanaedu.org

 778-668-7033

Manufactured by Amazon.ca
Bolton, ON